High Tolerance

High Tolerance
The Intoxicating World of Alcohol Marketing

Ella Parlor

All Rights Reserved. No portion of this book may be reproduced, stored in a retrieval system, or transmitted in any form or by any means – electronic, mechanical, photocopy, recording, scanning, or other – except for brief quotations in critical reviews or articles without the prior permission of the author.

Published by Game Changer Publishing

Paperback ISBN: 978-1-962656-00-9
Hardcover ISBN: 978-1-962656-01-6
Digital: ISBN: 978-1-962656-02-3

www.GameChangerPublishing.com

DISCLAIMER

Sip on This.

This book is the author's very own signature concoction of views and opinions based upon true events and reflects the author's spirited recollections of experiences over time.

Some names and characteristics have been muddled, events have been shaken and stirred, and dialogue has been crafted with a twist to maintain anonymity and privacy for all involved.

Similar to a cocktail umbrella, this book is not intended to provide shade to any organization, institution, or individual with whom the author has shared a drink or project.

As every alcohol commercial includes a disclaimer, please remember that neither the publisher nor any associated parties will be held responsible for any hangovers, unexpected party fouls, or consequences that may arise from the author's opinions or interpretations within these pages.

Please enjoy these literary libations responsibly!

DEDICATION

Hey Hey Hey,

Thank you for joining me on the journey highlighted in this book. Within these chapters, you'll uncover insights and strategies gleaned from my career collaborating with globally recognized brands in the food, beverage, and sports sectors.

Whether crafting multi-million dollar marketing plans, motivating sales teams, or coaching individuals one-on-one, my passion remains to empower others to tap into their brilliance.

As a business consultant and transformative coach, I'm committed to guiding others toward profound fulfillment, both professionally and personally.

Whether you're ambitious, feeling stuck, or in search of a fresh direction, I am here, hand-in-hand, to elevate you and believe in you!

Visit me at @ellayourbella or visit ellayourbella.com to discuss reframing your perspective today.

With gratitude and belief in your limitless potential,

Ella

High Tolerance

The Intoxicating World of Alcohol Marketing

Ella Parlor

www.GameChangerPublishing.com

Table of Contents

Introduction – Raising a Toast to the Alcohol Industry 1

Part One 9
Chapter 1 – The Boring Part of Booze: Laws & Regulations 11
Chapter 2 – From Barstools to Boardrooms: Climbing the Corporate Ladder .. 19
Chapter 3 – Win Or Lose, We Booze: Sports Marketing 33

Part Two 45
Chapter 4 – For the Culture: The Complexities of Multicultural Marketing 47
Chapter 5 – Behind the Spotlight: Celebrities and Influencers 63
Chapter 6 – My Career Cocktail: Strategy and Analytics 71

Part Three 77
Chapter 7 – Stirring Up Success: Leadership Development 79
Chapter 8 – Uncomfortably Numb: The Darker Side of Alcohol 91

Part Four 101
Chapter 9 – A Sobering Epiphany 103
Chapter 10 – Life After Alcohol: Finding Purpose Beyond the Bottle 119

INTRODUCTION

Raising a Toast to the Alcohol Industry

"I don't understand why you stopped drinking. Isn't that bad for…"

Don't say it. Don't you dare say it. I glared back at him from across the kitchen, wishing I could telepathically tape his whiskey-stained mouth shut. Right behind his beautiful head of luscious hair was a wooden cupboard full of various whiskey, tequila, and vodka brands I had worked with throughout the years, including a limited-edition bottle that had been discontinued several years ago. I swooned when he told me the story of how he found it at a restaurant in Las Vegas and had to order over ten drinks for himself, his friends, and neighboring tables to render it empty just so the bartender would let him take the bottle home. Ales, my handsome—and in this particular moment, sloppy—boyfriend, was the first man I ever dated who took a real interest in the work I do.

He, a design engineer, was fascinated and enthralled as we strolled down the aisles of his favorite liquor store; stories about various marketing campaigns I developed poured out of me while our fingers gently brushed across the glass bottles. He took such an interest in my work that he began a small collection of brands from my past and present. Although I couldn't see the bottles that were hidden behind his wooden kitchen cupboard at the moment, they radiated, pulsated, almost mocking me as he continued, "...Bad for business, Ella?"

I knew he was going to say that. Ales—short for Alessandro—was utterly unimpressed with my decision to stop drinking alcohol for thirty days and even went as far as to call me "boring" the evening prior when I refused to take shots with him at one of our usual hangouts. Today, he was extra peeved to discover that all the mimosas I drank at brunch did not, in fact, break my "boring" 10-day streak of alcohol abstinence because they were a mix of just pineapple juice, orange juice, and Sprite—a mock-mosa recipe I cleverly designed myself. And thanks to the tangy complexity of pineapple, they taste just as good as the real thing.

I wasn't offended or upset at Ales' absurd insinuation that my decision to stop drinking for a brief period of time could crumble the multi-billion-dollar industry in which I worked; I was concerned about the direction of the conversation. How would I ever open the door to ask him to stop drinking while simultaneously celebrating the 250% increase in sales my last digital campaign yielded for a gin brand I developed? My decision to stop drinking rendered him annoyed and uncomfortable. Perhaps he thought he had finally found a woman who would keep up with his travel and binge-drinking marathons. Admittedly, I can throw back whiskey and tequila with the best of them. Perhaps his interest in my career masked or pacified his fear of being exposed as the belligerent alcoholic I was beginning to ascertain that he was. For years, I have made a fabulous living convincing adults to drink particular cocktails or mixed beverages, and now I was unsure how to approach asking someone I love to stop.

Hello, my name is Ella Parlor, and I'm a marketing director in the alcohol industry. Well, I was a marketing director, and I am currently on sabbatical. Unlike a lawyer or doctor whose titles come from their education, not career output, I can't really call myself a marketing director if I stop working. "What do you do?" has always been a question that excites and terrifies me because many people do not understand what marketing is. I envy doctors, lawyers, teachers, nurses, bartenders, writers, truck drivers, and police officers because while people might not actually know what their jobs entail, they have a conceptualization, an idea of what they do. My career is often met with a confused, "So, you get paid to just give people free [insert whiskey, vodka, tequila, gin, beer, or beverage brand here]?" My work is fun, glamorous, gritty, difficult, beautiful, obscure, and puzzling.

Take, for instance, the cast of the popular television show *Friends*. We know that Monica is a chef, Ross is a professor and a paleontologist, Phoebe is an artist, Joey is an actor, and Rachel is a barista, but no one really knows what Chandler does. He has a job; he makes a decent living. But if you were to say, "What does he do? What is Chandler?" There isn't really a word for it besides businessman. When describing what it is I do, I wish I had one or two words the way most other professions do. The term "marketing director" is far too vague and only opens the door for more questions, so I've settled on "marketing director" in the alcohol industry," despite it being a mouthful. What do I do, exactly? Well, I've essentially been keeping America drunk since 2008.

A common follow-up question is often an excitable, "Oh, wow! How did you get into that?" I usually shrug it off as being a long story or oversimplify by explaining I had an internship during my college years. When I originally decided to pen this book, it was with the intention of answering those questions of who I am (professionally speaking), what I do, and how I got here.

Before I delve more deeply into who I am, it might also be an opportunity to offer who and what I am not, mostly because my attorneys and publisher said I ought to. I am not a lawyer; nothing in this book should be taken as credible legal advice. I am not a doctor, and the medical information offered in this book is closely tied to the scope of my specific experiences.

My intention is that you reconsider and re-evaluate your relationship with the alcohol industry because, whoever you are, you have one. Whether you drink alcohol, abstain from alcohol, identify as an alcoholic, or have a loved one with a drinking problem, you have a relationship with alcohol. Do you remember how pricey your high school prom tickets were? This was likely because prom venues factor in their usual alcohol sales into their rental fees, whether alcohol is served or not. So, chances are, you have funded the alcohol business in some capacity more than you realize.

After the 2020 pandemic, it is no secret we are overstimulated, with an overwhelming desire to desensitize and detach. I am not a therapist, a sober coach, or a member of Alcoholics Anonymous. I am also not sober. I love alcohol. I relish the sweet heat of a charred whiskey. I find melting small slivers of ice in a freshly shaken martini with my tongue exhilarating. This is not some live-your-best-sober-life anthem designed to stop you from drinking. In fact, half of this book was written while I was sitting in a bar under the influence of alcohol. After fifteen years of promoting alcoholic beverages for the world's largest booze brands, I am a far cry from sober. That said, if the consequence of this book is that I get sober or someone reads it and decides to drink less, I would say that is a step in the right direction because the ugly truth is we are drinking too much.

In the next ten years, we expect alcohol consumption to increase by 30% in the United States. 30%. According to a research study by the Grand View Research group, the revenue generated by RTDs (Ready-To-Drink, canned alcoholic mixed drinks) will grow by 13% by 2023, yielding 2.43 billion dollars in revenue. Bear in mind the population is only expected to grow by 2% in that time frame. Furthermore, not all of that population will be of legal drinking age. And so, what that means is for consumption to grow by 30% when the population is only growing by 2% is one of two things:

1. We, as advertisers in the alcohol space, are expecting adults to drink more alcohol tomorrow than they do today.

2. We anticipate adults not drinking today will start drinking for the first time.

Frankly, I find this alarming. Alcohol is one of the only substances on this planet that has its own diseases in human beings: liver disease, fetal alcohol syndrome, alcoholic hepatitis, certain types of cirrhosis, pancreatitis, and cancerous diseases. Lest we not forget the documented and clear correlation between alcohol and mental disorders such as depression, anxiety, PTSD, etc. I intend to offer a BTS (that's a TikTok way of saying behind-the-scenes, for you old cats) of the fast-changing laws and advertising affecting alcohol consumption today. While other industries are scaling back on their marketing and advertising budgets, alcohol is going full throttle, teetering on lines that have never been crossed before. According to a study by Zenith's Business Intelligence – Alcohol: Beer & Spirits, it is expected that alcohol companies will spend over $8.5 billion U.S. dollars on advertising in the US markets, surpassing ad spends pre-pandemic.

Today, I can't imagine how I would've felt 20, 15, or even 10 years ago, reading that as of today, in 2023, Jack and Cola is available in a can. Hello Kitty makes wine. Vodka and whiskey brands are building bars at college stadiums. Starbucks serves whiskey at certain locations. The list grows each day. Celebrities who don't even drink alcohol are buying brands and promoting them. Things that were illegal 10 or 15 years ago are taken for granted today. No, this is not a sobriety book. What I want to offer is insight into the alcohol industry from the inside as someone who, quite frankly, has made a career of influencing millions of people to consume certain products at certain times.

Really, the intention of this book is threefold:

1. Help you realize some of the trends within the alcohol space from a marketing and advertising perspective.

2. Examine and review some of the laws that affect alcohol consumption in the United States.

3. Provide an overview of the trajectory that seems to be unfolding regarding alcohol consumption in the US.

High Tolerance delves into the cultural nuances of alcohol consumption in the U.S., urging readers to reflect on our own relationships with alcohol and providing insights into both personal drinking habits and the broader impacts of alcohol advertising. At its core, it serves as a guide to brand growth, spotlighting innovative marketing tactics, market research, and strategies for media engagement, especially in the realm of social media. This book can also be a resource tailored for marketing professionals, students, policymakers, scholars, and anyone curious about the interplay between alcohol, advertising, and society.

Many people joke, "Band-Aids and rubbing alcohol for my outside boo-boos; alcohol for my inside boo-boos." My intention and ultimate hope are that we make conscious, healthy decisions and perhaps consider that it's time for all of us to drink less. Let's reevaluate cultural norms surrounding alcohol consumption and our hesitations to confront them.

PART ONE

Tolerance: The capacity of the body to endure or become less responsive to a substance, such as a drug, with repeated use or exposure.

Usage: *"That woman's tolerance is so high she can drink three tequila shots without even flinching."*

CHAPTER ONE

The Boring Part of Booze: Laws & Regulations

If you were to ask when my personal fascination with alcohol started, I would probably venture to guess that it began somewhere in my 20s, or maybe even my teen years, when my peers began experimenting with their parent's liquor cabinets. But as I recall various songs that I loved to sing as a child with lines like "Pass the Courvoisier," "Girls are on the way; where the Bacardi at?" and "Sippin' on Gin & Juice, laid back with my mind on my money and my money on my mind," alcohol has always been an aggrandized supporting character in my favorite music videos of the 1990s and early 2000s.

Reflecting on these jams, I remembered an assignment from seventh grade about the Amendments of the Constitution. My teacher, Mr. Grayson, assigned one amendment to each student. But when it came to me, he assigned me two amendments, the 18th and 21st. I was appalled and annoyed. Vexed and eager to call it out, my hand shot up into the air. "Excuse me, Mr. Grayson, why do I get two amendments when everybody else only gets one? That's not fair!"

He chuckled, "I had a feeling you'd react this way, but something tells me you'll be able to handle it." He added, "If you do the assignment, maybe you'll understand."

And so, I undertook the assignment and came to learn about the 18th Amendment. Now, if you're not a history buff, I don't blame you. I wouldn't fancy myself one either, but I do enjoy knowing the history of something, especially something to which I've dedicated my entire career. The 18th Amendment is famously known as the Prohibition Amendment. It prohibited the manufacturing, sale, and transportation of alcoholic beverages in the United States in 1920 and introduced the ever-popular concept of speakeasies in this country.

One of the biggest bragging points I have about working in the alcohol industry is that it trumps most other industries. Let's be real. Very few industries are associated with such negative connotations as death and destruction. You have the pharma industry, the arms trade industry, the tobacco industry, and, in my controversial opinion, even the food industry. But what we in the alcohol sector have that no other industry boasts are two amendments in the Constitution. Not one, but two.

And so I learned that the 18th Amendment essentially eradicated alcohol in this country. My project about prohibition featured pictures of 1920s flappers, underground speakeasies, Al Capone, and discussions about what we today recognize as prohibition. Thirteen years after its enactment, the 18th Amendment, uniquely making it the only amendment to be rescinded, was repealed in 1933 by the 21st Amendment. This allowed the legal distribution, sale, and consumption of alcoholic beverages once again in the United States.

I hold a somewhat uncomfortable and perhaps conspiratorial belief that the repeal of alcohol prohibition was not due to concerns about the puritanical values that spurred the prohibition movement but rather an interest in generating revenue through taxation. Is it a coincidence that the 21st Amendment, which decriminalized alcohol, was passed in 1933 during the Great Depression? I don't think so. With the enactment of the 21st Amendment, certain new laws came into effect, which had a major impact on the taxation of alcohol (taxes, so many taxes.)

Why mention this? Well, alcohol taxes affect the business from top to bottom, with consumers ultimately footing the bill. Moreover, the various regulations (and the governing agencies that enforce them) impact my job as a marketer every single day.

Have you ever wondered why you can't stroll the streets with an open container of alcohol? Well, the answer, at least from my observation, is taxes. The government is perfectly fine with you drinking yourself to oblivion as long as they get their pay, and you, of course, don't physically harm anyone by participating in reckless behavior such as driving, fighting, etc. In fact, I will take this a step further; I believe it's our government's best interest that we drink (more on that in a bit).

To elaborate, I first will need to dissect the very complex system created by the 21st Amendment, which is known as the 3-tier system. When you note the term "3-tier system," it's a fancy industry term that means "booze bizz."

At the risk of oversimplifying, here is my breakdown of the 3-tier system and how the government benefits from it:

Let's say you and I decide to start a whiskey company, and one bottle of our whiskey costs us $1 to produce. That makes us the manufacturer, producer, supplier, and the first tier of the alcohol industry.

Now, thanks to the 21st Amendment, we cannot sell our bottle to regular folks on the street; we have to sell our whiskey to the second tier, a wholesaler or distributor (these mean the exact same thing), and we have to pay $0.50 in taxes for producing the liquor. So, we sell our bottle of whiskey to a wholesaler for $2.50, giving us a $1 profit.

When the wholesaler or 2nd tier purchases our product, they also have to pay taxes, so they actually bought it for $3. Now, they also want to make a profit, so they sell it to the third tier for $4. The third tier includes all retailers, liquor stores, restaurants, etc., who also have to pay taxes, so they purchase the bottle for $5. Retailers, of course, need to make a profit when selling to consumers, so they sell the liquor to their consumers for $7, and the consumer ends up paying $8 with taxes. So, instead of us being able to sell our $1 bottle of whiskey to consumers ourselves for $2-3, the consumers are paying $8 a bottle, absorbing the cost of profits and taxes.

To add some complexity for thought, this 3-tier system means you and I do not just sell our whiskey once; we have to sell it three times just to get our $1 profit and repeat business.

So, as a marketer working directly for the brands and suppliers in the first tier, it is my job to create external campaigns and advertisements that excite not just the consumers at the end of the funnel but also my wholesalers and retailer partners.

The 3-tier system's intricacy makes the first tier, the supplier level, extremely challenging to enter. Many aspire to work directly for alcohol manufacturers, but navigating the intricate regulations is daunting for those who are unfamiliar with these complexities. In chapter four, I delve deeper into my observations of hiring trends within the wine and spirit industry.

And in case you thought my $1 whiskey example was a bit of an exaggeration, in my experience, the average production cost of a 750ML bottle of liquor is about $5-$10, and the average shelf price is around $20-50. According to Statista.com and The 2022 Beer Serves America Report, the federal government collected $9.9 Billion in excise taxes from beer, wine, and liquor sales in 2020. And that's not including local and state governments. It is also predicted that that number will rise closer to $11 Billion by 2023. So, cheers to funding our government, one sip at a time.

Now, what does Uncle Sam do with all this tax money? Well, I cannot say for sure. However, a law isn't really a law if there is no one to enforce it. That's why there have been times when I've had to work with or cooperate with various law enforcement agencies. Here are the agencies that I have encountered or worked with as a marketing director:

1. Alcohol and Tobacco Tax and Trade Bureau (TTB)

The TTB is a bureau under the Department of Treasury. This is who I've worked with the most. When I say "work with," I'm really just saying that I'm filling out paperwork for them or receiving correspondence from them either through my legal or executive teams, never directly speaking with them myself. I've managed various tasks, requests, and permits that the TTB requires. The TTB enforces federal laws related to the production, distribution, labeling, advertising, and, you guessed it, taxation of alcohol. This is why I like to talk about taxes because if you're drinking alcohol, you are paying them out the wazoo.

And not all alcoholic beverages are taxed the same. And so sometimes, when we're deciding to even start a whole new brand line or innovation, we will consider the tax implications of foreign exports and laws. *The Presidential Administration just added 25% tariffs to French products, so we should stay away from Cognac right now.* There are laws that U.S. presidents, the Senate, and Congress enact directly shape our day-to-day work.

2. Food and Drug Administration (FDA)

I've had limited dealings with the FDA, as they typically defer to the TTB for most alcohol brands. They mainly intervene with hard seltzers concerning health claims on labels. Legally, alcoholic beverages can't make health claims. So, while you might feel more energetic after a drink, don't expect a vodka label to promise better workouts or lowered blood pressure. Sure, some hard seltzers advertise electrolytes akin to sports drinks. But let's be clear: no alcoholic drink, even with added electrolytes, offers health benefits. Period.

3. Alcoholic Beverage Control (ABC)

Ah, the State ABC - the self-appointed fun police. While I've never crossed paths with anyone from the mysterious TTB, our friends at the ABC make their presence felt locally, and not in a good way. These are the guys who go undercover looking to bust bartenders who don't ask for an ID and charge astronomical fines.

If you have ever seen a snazzy beer or whiskey neon sign at your favorite bar, odds are, it's breaking some obscure ABC law and could be about a $3,000 fine. Sometimes, sales and marketing teams have to roll the dice by making less-than-legal advertising materials for our retailers. Of course, we want to be responsible and want our consumers to be responsible. Morally, we would never condone a campaign that promotes underage or excessive drinking. Not only is it unethical, but those fines for that are so astronomical that they can destroy an entire business. Those are not the type of laws I'm talking about breaking here. I am talking about giving out branded cups (yes, cups!) being illegal. Who doesn't love an alcohol-branded pint glass, beer stein, or copper mule mug? Make it make sense, ABC. Sometimes, it seems these tedious laws are designed with the sole intention of more fines and dollars for Uncle Sam. Like I said, bureaucratic beverage fun police.

4. Federal Trade Commission (FTC)

My few encounters with the FTC have been unnerving. You never want them on your line, no matter your industry. In the alcohol sector, they closely monitor sweepstakes because sweepstakes are a significant part of our advertising and consumer engagement tactics. If you break the strict sweepstakes rules, the FTC will quickly find you.

5. Bureau of Alcohol, Tobacco, Firearms and Explosives (ATF)

These guys are flat-out terrifying. They are the alcohol, tobacco, and firearm equivalent of Homeland Security and a segment within the Department of Justice. They are hardcore. They mostly don't worry about alcohol companies operating legally, such as the brands I've worked for. I've actually encountered them only once, and we were the plaintiffs.

A company I worked for was having problems with bootleg and black-market products and coupons being distributed in North America through my territory in Long Beach, CA. The fact that there are people who make fake, knock-off versions of alcohol brands is more terrifying than the ATF agents who bust them. A counterfeit Louie-Louie-Fendi-Prada purse might be cute, but drinking some chemical connotation made in a warehouse with zero QA can be outright lethal. Prayerfully, the ATF does not mess around or waste any time with those sickos. They are real-life superheroes.

6. Consumer Product Safety Commission (CPSC)

Not only are these guys the easiest to work with, but they also have the lowest fines and fees. The CPSC ensures that various bottles, packaging, and promotional items are safe. For example, those illegally branded cups I mentioned need to be toxic-free and safe to mix with alcohol. Straightforward and easy-going, they are probably my favorite.

Beyond the government, other councils regulate the alcohol industry's business practices. For example, champagne, scotch, tequila, bourbon, and cognac have specific legal definitions from specific regions worldwide.

By now, you might be thinking, *This is getting tedious and boring. I thought alcohol was supposed to be fun!* While fun, the world of alcohol marketing is incredibly complex and interdisciplinary. It encompasses law, regulations, policy, business economics, media, mass communications, psychology, behavioral sciences, public health, sociology, cultural studies, data science, and research.

This is why when people ask, "What do you do?" and "How did you get that role?" My answer is inconsistent and all over the place. To be successful in alcohol marketing, you must enjoy cross-functional environments and adapt to various personalities and challenges, all while building creative, energetic, innovative campaigns.

CHAPTER TWO

From Barstools to Boardrooms: Climbing the Corporate Ladder

As a marketer, you are, in essence, in every room, making sure that your business unit remains a well-lubricated machine. While my career progression is perhaps my favorite love story, riddled with triumphs, celebrations, and setbacks, I find the persistent question of "How did you get into this?" a bit weighted.

The foundation of my career was laid years before my first marketing internship in college. Technically, my first job was when I was three years old, going to the playground and directing the other children on what they could play on and when. Naturally, my brother got first dibs on any structure he wanted. Another early "job" was in kindergarten when I sold invisible dresses to other students, who would give me food or money in exchange. I got into significant trouble for that one. In retrospect, I feel like my entrepreneurial genius was undermined, but that's a story for my therapist.

When I was in fifth grade, my great aunt, a nurse who volunteered at convalescent homes, used to drag my brother, my cousins, and me along with her. She instilled the importance of caring for the elderly, a passionate belief I still hold today. My cousin played the piano, while I would try out various vocalizing and dance moves I learned from Britney Spears's music videos. That was the first and last season of my life where I would receive a standing ovation for my singing and dancing. It probably didn't hurt that our audience couldn't see or hear too well.

In school, I won every essay contest I entered, which likely explains my knack for copywriting and internal communications today. Revisiting the story of Mr. Greyson's amendments assignments, I often challenged authority growing up, leading many teachers to find me (let's say) petulant. One teacher even compared me to Stalin, to which I quickly retorted, "Stalin basically took down Hitler, so I'm not offended by that comparison."

By the time I learned about mean, median, and mode in 7th-grade algebra, I realized that people, like numbers, can tell whatever story you want if you know how to position and analyze them—the exact same dataset and facts can tell several different stories.

My very first official job, one recognized by the IRS due to tax deductions, was at Hula Harbor, a laid-back coastal-themed burger joint I still frequent today. I owe this opportunity to my dear friend Emma, who recommended me for the position when I had unsuccessfully applied to other restaurants. Emma herself had landed the job, thanks to her older sister's recommendation, and this experience revealed a profound business lesson and insight: your reputation and referrals are crucial in unlocking business opportunities.

Before heading to work at Hula Harbor, I would go to Vita Vibe, a smoothie shop next door. Occasionally, the manager would ask, "Would you like to work here?" At first, I wasn't particularly interested because Vita shared tips via one tip jar, versus the cash tips I earned during each shift at Hula. However, one evening at Hula, I asked to leave early due to severe period cramps, and my boss accused me of just wanting to party. I responded with a less-than-graceful farewell by flipping the bird and moonwalking backward out of the restaurant, an idea inspired by Drew Barrymore's character in the 2000 movie, *Charlie's Angels*. While I welcome challenges to my ideas, I don't appreciate being accused of lying when I say I need time off for health reasons.

The next day, I found myself at Vita Vibe, taking the manager up on her offer for a new job. *Nepotism—gotta love it.*

One of the beauties—and sometimes pains—of working in Southern California is that many executives find reasons to visit. Between the beautiful weather and big footprint events like Coachella, the Oscars, and the Grammys, executives of each company I have worked for have always found an excuse to visit Southern California. Sometimes they would announce their arrival, and other times they would "secret shop."

I, too, have gone *undercover* to various pop-up shops, events, and accounts to gain qualitative feedback and gauge the success of a campaign I helped build. I relish asking a bartender, who is entirely unaware I created it, how they found the T-shirt they are wearing and what they think about it. As a marketer, being incognito has been a secret weapon, enabling me to receive unfiltered feedback and keep my thumb on the pulse of market trends.

Many times, I have stood adjacent to the main bar at a concert venue and approached someone after their drink purchase, inquiring, "Where did you get that?" "What's it called?" "Is it good?" Unaware I designed the cocktail names and menu, they offer sincere, frank feedback. One of the issues I have with brand marketing teams is that we sit perched around a conference room, patting each other on the back for a job well done, because our work *feels* good when presented as a concept.

Where I observe several brands, campaigns, and strategies go wrong is that what is conceptualized in a polished boardroom does not always translate properly to the end user. This is why so many campaigns flop or receive unexpected backlash. For me, attending events and getting live, real-time feedback from consumers, the heart of our business, is educational, humbling, and exciting. When someone says to me, "This cocktail is incredible, you have to try it!" and even adds some educational takeaway, my heart is delighted. It is a true joy that eclipses any accolades from a colleague or VP.

Throughout my career, I've been secret-shopped by HQ executives, probably more often than I even realize. Far from perfect, I strive to do my best in every job every day, assuming someone is always watching. This may sound a bit ominous, but I have actually found it to be overwhelmingly beneficial for me. TV shows like *Undercover Boss* and *Secret Millionaire*, coupled with my deep-seated desire to exceed expectations, mean that I try to treat everybody as though they are the CEO or the CEO's child.

Consequently, I tend to go above and beyond in the name of customer service, client relations, account management, leadership, or team development. So, when there have been times that I was under a microscope of which I was unaware, I have (to my knowledge) overperformed and impressed upper management, receiving rave reviews and feedback for my work.

I first experienced this when I was sixteen, working as a hostess at Hula Harbor. My role was probably the most expendable, as servers could seat themselves, and big rushes or wait times only occurred a couple of times a week. That said, I wanted to be a server and jumped at any opportunity to act as one. If a server was slammed, I'd take their tables' drink orders and hand them to the server directly. Was it a bit out of my job description? Yes, but I know how it feels to be a restaurant guest, a client, waiting for anyone to acknowledge you, so I overstepped a bit as a hostess to make the guest experience more pleasant and save the server some time. This felt like a win-win to me.

So when Mark Balboa, owner of Hula Harbor, came into the restaurant, he got the exact same treatment I gave every other table. I had no idea who he was, a sentiment he realized and echoed to my manager, "You could tell she had no clue who I was." He gave an enthusiastic review, and my manager was thrilled it happened in her store.

A couple of years later, I found a tip hack while making smoothies at Vita Vibe. Back in the early 2000s, people still paid for goods and services with this funny, smelly paper called cash. Since the smoothies cost exactly $5, adding a $0.25 boost meant they would likely drop their coin change in the tip jar. So, I made it my personal mission to upgrade folks' smoothies with a boost.

"I noticed you just worked out. Do you want a protein boost to help with your muscle recovery today?" "Oh, my zest comes from the energy boost I added to my smoothie this morning—they're only 25 cents!"

So when the Vita Vibe corporate team secretly visited me, they received the same boost spiel I gave to every customer.

The next day, I was called into my manager's office—an experience that continues to evoke an unsettling feeling in my gut to this day. These encounters, although typically positive, still fill me with apprehension. I harbor this irrational fear that I am going to be terminated on the spot for a sin I didn't know I committed. This feeling is hauntingly reminiscent of being summoned to the principal's office.

I imagine that this fear of rejection after falling short of perfectionism traces back to my childhood. Growing up, my father's scrutiny of my homework was relentless, and at times, he would rip it to shreds, forcing me to start over from scratch. Bear in mind, this was in the old days of the late 1900s when folks still wrote their homework by hand with a prehistoric tool called a pencil. I know my father is looking down right now, smiling, proud of himself for being the driving force behind my unyielding pursuit of perfection. He is not dead, my father. I just assume he's looking down on this book while reading it like most humans do.

It turns out I wasn't being fired; I was being promoted to the Vita Vibe marketing team to serve smoothie samples at events. *FREE smoothie samples. Are you kidding me?* With an hourly raise of $5, I was free from handling cash and explaining costs. Plus, I could enjoy unlimited samples, avoiding the sneaky tastes we would steal at the storefront. Stealing is wrong, but throwing away a perfectly good smoothie because a customer changed her mind about it never sat right with me.

It was on our smoothie blender bus that I developed a relationship with the national tour manager, Pamela, in whom I confided my secret desire to work at Tastey's one day. Tastey's was a beachy sports bar where the female servers wore tight t-shirts and booty shorts. I was never interested in being a model or actress, but for whatever reason, getting hired at Tastey's, an iconic restaurant known for its beauty and glamor, satisfied some Dolly Parton nostalgia I harbored.

Pamela's eyes widened, "Are you kidding me? Tastey's? Honey, I worked there when I was in college, and let me tell you, those girls are my lifelong friends to this day!"

My Vita Vibe manager continued to rave about the ambiance, the music, the flattering uniforms, and the body positivity.

As I looked beyond her glasses and noted her long blonde hair pulled up by a clip, I could see that this businesswoman was, in fact, gorgeous underneath the plain Jane façade she brought to work. I was in shock—this woman worked in corporate America. "Aren't you afraid people will find out and judge you for having worked at Tastey's?"

"Oh honey," she chuckled, "Anyone who judges me for putting myself through college by working at a family restaurant in broad daylight was probably never good-looking enough to work there in the first place."

"Am I good-looking enough? I won't even be eighteen for another couple of months."

"Oh, baby girl, you are gorgeous. Are you kidding me? You're only young once; go try out. I know you're going to shine! And if you don't like it, you can always come back to this little juice gem."

And off to Tastey's I went, ignoring the critical feedback I got from friends and family. While bouncing around as a Tastey's Girl was as fun as I imagined, I didn't expect to be so damn proud of my work there. Despite the whispers and murmurs from others in my small Catholic community, I knew deep down that there was something very valuable about working at Tastey's. Not only did I experience personal growth and gain confidence during my tenure, but I also learned how to network with individuals, including various executives. I developed stellar communication skills, cultivated a strong work ethic, and gained a level of financial independence that I otherwise would not have had at that age. Additionally, I was in an environment that promoted body positivity before it became a trendy hashtag on Instagram. I had a flexible school and work schedule, and overall, Tastey's provided numerous positive memories and experiences. Furthermore, a piece of Tastey's that I carry with me to this day is a dedication to stellar and excellent client services. I also love that I worked at Tastey's because it was probably one of the first adult decisions I made in my life, without my parents' blessing, carving out how I wanted to show up in this world.

If it's not clear by now, every single job I have had directly led me to my next role and/or promotion. A friend referred me to Hula Harbor, which led me to Vita Vibe next door. That is where I met Pamela, who encouraged me to apply at Tastey's. This experience played a crucial role in my jump into beverage marketing.

Today, I have sat in several meetings with various Sales Directors, discussing cocktail menus, programs, and advertising for various chain restaurants, including Tastey's. Sometimes, a new or immature colleague will crack a lame joke or snicker. I am always amused by the reaction I get when I interject, "What's so funny? I used to work there." Like Pamela from Vita Vibe, I have zero shame about my time at Tastey's. It was an incredible experience that shaped the foundation of my career today.

Many of the women I worked with at that restaurant have since become wildly successful in various fields, becoming NASA engineers, teachers, lawyers, doctors, mothers, and business owners. Despite our varying paths, we Tastey's girls all have something in common—we work our tails off and have serious grit. So, hell yes, I will always be proud that I worked at Tastey's.

For one, it was the first job I had where I would wake up in the morning excited to go to work—it was a literal dream job. I got paid to watch sports, talk smack, and serve beer. Fast forward to today, and my job in the alcohol industry still consists of watching sports, talking smack, and serving drinks.

At our Tastey's location, sandwiched between two sports arenas, we hosted celebrities, athletes, and brand managers. One day, a brand ambassador taught us about a new product called Huntsman Liqueur, a key ingredient in the popular Herbal Bomb cocktail. I learned Herbal Bombs were made with High Octane, my favorite energy drink. Before this, I'd never thought of it as an alcohol mixer.

I was still under the legal drinking age and did not know the ins and outs of cocktails or drinking rituals. All I knew was that just like upselling smoothie boosts at Vita Vibe, selling more beer or liquor meant bigger tips. So, I pushed Herbal Bombs. I experimented with different serving styles and shot techniques, making the night memorable for consumers, who would later return requesting to sit in my section. I treated my section as my own mini enterprise, driving sales and delightful experiences to gain loyalty and repeat business. Unlike other servers who whined about getting too many customers in their section at once, I welcomed being double, triple, or quadruple-sat. I treated my tables as real estate rentals and aimed to maximize my earnings by flipping my tables as quickly as possible.

During my tenure at Tastey's, Jefe Tequila and Huntsman were the only two brands that offered educational trainings for our team. And guess what I sold the most? Jefe Tequila and Huntsman, because that's all I knew. This experience is why, in later roles as a marketing manager, I have incorporated brand ambassadors and educational classes into brand budgets. As a brand, educating your end consumer alone will not suffice to push your product down the funnel; educational programs for your retailers and partners ensure that they act as extensions of your brand, advocating for and promoting it, just as I did as a Tastey's server.

Despite popular belief, Tastey's was not the easiest job, and one of the hardest parts was making it look easy. Tastey's had a system called Ops 19, which outlined the 19 expectations for guest interactions with every meal, every table, every single day. The list of expectations included greeting your guests within 30 seconds, offering fries with every meal, repeating their order aloud, suggesting a dessert, etc. If you got secret-shopped and missed any of the 19 expectations, you were fired.

One night during a big UFC fight, a group of teenage girls sat in my section. Tastey's seemed an odd choice for a group of girls on a Friday night, and I was even more surprised when they left me a very generous tip of 50%. The next day, I was pulled into my manager's office. As a server with the top food, beverage, and merchandise sales, I was confident I was about to receive good news. This marks the first (and likely last) time I walked into a manager's office assuming the news would be positive. It turns out those teenage girls were secret shoppers. And while their report gave positive qualitative feedback, they indicated that I didn't offer fries.

To this day, several years later, I swear to you, I offered those damn fries. It was extremely loud, and maybe they didn't hear me, but I offered them. Nevertheless, per policy, I was fired on the spot. I wonder if those girls knew the implication of checking that little box. How often is it that we make a flippant comment or small action that echoes and shatters the world of another? I was devastated. It felt like an awful breakup. "Who gets fired from Tastey's?" my father scoffed, disappointed in the termination and the reasoning behind it.

A friend learned about me getting fired and said, "Hey, come work at this nightclub as a VIP host." For the first time, I was amidst lavish lifestyles and extravagant displays of wealth congruent with the nightlife scene. It was the first time in my life that I saw people openly use illicit drugs and spend thousands of dollars in cash without batting an eye.

One night, a beautiful bottle service girl bragged in the back kitchen that someone had given her a Lamborghini as a tip. We stood in utter disbelief as she held the keys, explaining that her customer was from Dubai and had purchased it while on vacation in the USA. He was unable to take the car back home for legal reasons and told her he would gladly transfer the title to her name. The restaurant owner, our boss, explained that she would have to turn over the Lamborghini for tax reasons, as it technically belonged to the restaurant. She didn't miss a beat; she shook her head and said, "Oh, okay, but can I just hold the keys tonight to pressure my other tables to tip better?" Our boss laughed and said that would be fine. We never saw her again. It took us about thirty minutes to realize she had taken off with the Lamborghini and would never return. It was all anyone could talk about the rest of the night. I remember thinking, *Oh my gosh, that girl is a straight-faced genius.* Had that been me at that time, at my young age, I would have just done whatever my boss asked. "Oh, I have to give you this Lamborghini that was given to me because of the IRS? Sure, here you go." Wherever that woman is in the world today, Godspeed, lady. Godspeed.

Hiding in the shadows of the nightclub was really fun at the beginning of my career, but it also came with some uncomfortable experiences. Once, I was propositioned for sex by an elderly couple. A middle-aged woman handed me a blank check for $2,500, saying, "My husband has been watching you all night and was wondering if you'd be interested in coming home with us." She nodded in the direction of a decrepit man, shaking in his walker, giving a half-hearted wave.

"Sorry, ma'am, I'm a virgin," I said with complete honesty and pity for the Newport Beach housewife. She was in her mid-fifties and gorgeous. It felt gross, sad, and humiliating to witness the wife of a man who would put her in such a position, asking a woman less than half her age to enter their marital bed. *I'd rather be single and poor*, I thought to myself.

Luckily, my stint as a VIP host was brief. The nightclub I worked for was a top account for High Octane, an energy drink, attracting regular visits from their sales reps. After casually mentioning my proficiency in Spanish to one of them, I received an invitation to interview with the brand.

Upon arriving at the High Octane office, I was tickled to discover that one of the panel's interviewers was the former Huntsman's Liqueur representative who had educated me on the brand at Tastey's! Her eyes lit up as I expressed how grateful I was for that brand training and how I leveraged the brand facts to drive more visibility and sales for Huntsman's.

An Englishwoman on the panel asked if I knew Spanish. I shared that my mother was born in Mexico and that I had studied the language in both high school and college. I was stunned when she replied in a British accent, "Muy bien, hagamos la entrevista en español," leading to the first of many Spanish interviews in my career.

I was hired and worked at High Octane during my undergraduate years. When graduation came, I was given a promotion and a raise, which was a big deal for any graduate following the recession of 2008.

While I was not immune to the challenges and uncertainties that come with entering "the real world" after college, working through school set me apart from my peers who didn't. While I had compassion for my friends who struggled post-graduation, I also took pride in the sacrifices I made, juggling a full-time job, a 3.7 GPA, and a social life during my studies.

I would emphasize to anyone young and/or in good health: give your best effort today and produce quality work to secure your future. While I still consider myself energetic, I can't match the intensity and pace with which I built my career foundation in my teens and twenties, balancing responsibilities, work travel, school, a social life, and sleepless nights. I believe that healthy individuals should push their limits to develop a strong work ethic, cultivate resilience, and establish a solid reputation.

As much as I'd like to credit my career successes to hard work alone, the truth is that almost every job I have landed came via a friend or colleague inside the company. **Your reputation matters**. I have come to understand and witness that networking is crucial for career mobility, and nepotism is alive and well in most recruitment practices. That's why I wish education focused more on the practical implications of building a solid network and productive habits. I am so very grateful for the various allies—usually women—in this space who have offered me opportunities to which I would not have otherwise been privy. I delve more deeply into the power of advocacy and mentorship in Chapters Four and Seven. Undoubtedly, my career would not be where it is today if I had relied on online job searches and cold-calling.

A few months into my promotion at High Octane, I was recruited to work at a huge vodka company. At the time, my heart was still hoping to get a full-time sales manager role with High Octane; working for an alcohol brand felt a bit provocative for me. But as I researched the vodka brand on Google in preparation for the interview, I was bewildered to discover a Black female executive had rebranded the vodka by hiring big-name rap and hip-hop artists to elevate its brand to luxury. The article then continued to talk about pricing strategies, a concept I had yet to encounter at the time but have grown to leverage throughout my career. Something about seeing a Black female executive work at the organization, whether she was still there or not, struck me—excited me. At the time, I had never even seen a Black manager, leader, or executive in any of the companies I worked for.

Something about that (and the fact that I would be paid nearly triple what I made at High Octane) was enough for me to pioneer a role I did not want. Despite my hesitation at the time, I look back so fondly on how innocent I was, unaware that I was forging my dream career.

There's a wonderful quote by Martin Luther King, "Take the first step in faith. You don't have to see the whole staircase, just take the first step."

Getting invited to join former colleagues at that first vodka company, which has since generated over $6 Billion in sales, was far more monumental than I ever imagined.

CHAPTER THREE

Win Or Lose, We Booze: Sports Marketing

Football is, and always has been, my favorite sport. I love the strategy, the planning, the leadership, teamwork, adaptability, agility, and performance under pressure. Football requires serious skills, specialization, excellence, celebrating achievements, and fierce determination; I can turn just about any life circumstance into a football analogy.

Arguably, my love of sports, especially American football, runs through my veins. My dad's cousin Charlie won a Super Bowl championship in 1983. My mother's older brother played football at Harvard University with a prestigious full-ride scholarship. I cherish memories of rallying behind my favorite uncle, her youngest brother, during his college matches. The energy was palpable. As a small toddler, I would sit, shivering on chilly metal benches, eagerly screaming with everyone else without truly understanding the game. All I knew was that football felt like magic. My uncles—my mother's brothers—were hometown heroes at Servite High School in Orange County, California. Servite stands shoulder-pad-to-shoulder-pad with California high school football powerhouses like Mater Dei, Bosco, and Long Beach Poly.

As an adult, while working in NFL spaces, if the question of my alma mater arises, I am quick to declare my allegiance to Servite High School. More often than not, my white lie is met with an enthusiastic nod and praise for Servite's exceptional football program. Yet occasionally, I encounter a curious tilt of the head with the question, "Isn't that an all-boys school?"

Okay, yes, Servite is an all-boys school, and I *technically* did not go there. But, I am an alumna of Servite's sister all-girls school, Rosary Academy. Rosary didn't have a football team, and Servite didn't have a cheerleading squad. Our cheerleaders wore "Servite" cheer uniforms to their football games—same same, but different.

It should also be noted that, despite my cheery disposition, I have never been a cheerleader—not because I didn't want to, but because my father wouldn't allow it. That's a story for another book.

Nevertheless, a surge of unyielding pride coursed through my veins as I stood on the sidelines during my years at Rosary, passionately cheering on the Servite football players. In my senior year, I couldn't come up with a Halloween costume, so I decided last minute to dress up as our high school's star fullback, Michael Williams. His girlfriend at the time approached me in a very unimpressed manner and asked why I was dressing up like a man—her boyfriend—for Halloween. I replied, "It's mid-season. He's a really good football player, and I thought it would be cool to dress up like him because he's like a mini superhero."

She had a hard time believing I was just a fan who liked football. It was easier to believe that I was trying to steal her man. She grossly underestimated the extent of my social awkwardness, especially in high school. If I had a crush on a guy named Barry, I would have probably avoided strawberries and raspberries to maintain a façade of a berry-free life. So let the record reflect that if I did have a crush on Mike, the last thing I would have done was dress up like him for Halloween.

To this day, my love of football puzzles people, which I imagine has something to do with the fact that I'm a woman. A guy wears a jersey, and other men give him a high-five. But when a woman wears a jersey, we are met with interrogations and accusations of being interested in the sport for reasons other than the love of the game. Never mind that I have partnered with more than twenty professional and college football teams in my career on behalf of various vodka, rum, and whiskey brands.

My role at Tastey's (a sports bar) was the first where it was quite literally my job to keep up with current sports events, news, trades, and more.

At Tastey's, part of the Ops 19 expectations was sitting down and speaking to every single customer for at least three minutes. It was crucial that I stayed up-to-date with happenings in football, basketball, hockey, baseball, college sports, and UFC, which was rapidly growing in popularity at that time. Sandwiched between sports arenas in Southern California, my time at Tastey's offered me valuable insights into the business of sports marketing, including partnerships, appearances, and branding.

If California were its own nation, it would have the second-highest number of professional basketball, football, baseball, and hockey teams in the world, with some teams even sharing venues.

Having several teams in one region means that fandom in California is often fair-weathered and contingent on a team's performance. Consequently, Californian teams face fierce competition with each other for sponsors and advertisers.

This is a dynamic many brands fail to understand when pursuing team partnerships in the California market. Certain marketing strategies that work in Wisconsin or Europe are not as effective in a saturated market like California.

To date, I have executed co-branded activations for SoCal teams like the Angels, Dodgers, Ducks, and Kings, but managing a partnership with the Los Angeles Lakers was truly a dream come true.

During my first on-site Lakers meeting, I was searching for our conference room, which was across the offices of Jeanie Buss and Magic Johnson—no big deal. I was late, and the door was locked. I frantically tried to open the door in different ways, and boom, it swung open. A man about seven feet tall towered over me and remarked, "It's a heavy door." As I noticed basketball players getting physical therapy and practicing their three-pointer shots, I realized I was not in the right room and had just barged into the Lakers' practice.

I found myself in the jarring position of being the only woman in the room, a situation I've encountered multiple times in my career. A different player approached me kindly, "Do you need help?"

Dear God, get me out of here. My heart was pounding, and I was still running late for my meeting. Quick on my feet and coping well under pressure, I blurted, "No, I'm fine. Just surveying the floor." I walked the entire perimeter of their practice court, nodded to the coaches, and pretended to take notes on my phone. What notes is anyone making about a floor? I don't know. I sprinted out the heavy door, sweating off any deodorant I had applied that day. Sometimes, it feels like things like this only happen to me.

Working with the NBA is not for the faint of heart. While each pro league has its nuances, the NBA is particularly hands-on with their team franchises. This is why my ability to plan, build, and execute the first-ever NBA social media campaign with a spirit brand is one of my top career highlights. By leveraging an already existing brand partnership with a franchise team, the social media campaign I built yielded over 6 million impressions and reached 3 million people.

To put that into perspective, a social media campaign with those results would cost a brand well over $100,000—I made it happen for "free." No spirit brand had ever done that before. Bear in mind, the campaign itself had other expenses for our brand. First, we already had a paid agreement that allowed us to use the team's logo. We also had to pay influencers and send them products. When I say the campaign was free, it is because no incremental money was given to the team to make the posts. Once again, absolutely nothing I have done in my career has been alone. A tremendous amount of teamwork from several agencies, partners, and coworkers was required. The campaign came to fruition through the power of well-crafted briefs, knowing how to scrutinize a partnership contract, and my relationships. Relationship building is crucial for any business and happens to be my not-so-secret weapon in making things happen, even at the risk of breaking a few rules.

Forever influenced by the marketing tactics I learned at High Octane, guerilla marketing will always harbor a special place in my scope of work. Guerilla marketing thrives in the world of sports because the fans, the athletes, and the outcomes of the games are so unpredictable.

While working for a beer brand, the World Series was hosted in my territory. Our biggest competitor was the beer sponsor of both teams, but we had a partnership with the stadium's hospitality vendor. Through the power of a solid relationship, our team strategically placed our beer in the laundry baskets of both clubhouses, unsure which team would win the game. The result? Our beer, in all its frothy glory, splashed across the front pages, showering the triumphant team. This, of course, was likely infuriating for our competitor. I almost feel bad. But in the marketing game, your product must be in the right place at the right time. Seeding our product into the winning team's clubhouse was a risky venture, but it was worth the end result. Every now and then, I still Google those images for giggles.

I am often asked how many athletes I have worked with in a marketing capacity, and the answer is underwhelming. Most of the athlete-specific sponsorships I observed were during my tenure at High Octane. While regulations are always changing, based on my experience and understanding, athletes in traditional sports are not permitted to have spirit brand partnerships until they retire. I assume this rationale lies in the unpredictable nature of individual athletes' behavior. Some athletes have a documented history of alcohol abuse, driving under the influence, and committing crimes. This poses a substantial liability concern for alcohol brands, sports teams, and the leagues.

Working with a mainstream athlete for the first time presented a significant learning curve for our team. We were all incredibly excited when he was about to play in the Super Bowl, convinced we could leverage the spotlight to drive more visibility for our brand. We had the rights to display his face in our promotions, but we couldn't use his NFL team's logo or the terms "Super" or "Bowl" since we weren't officially partnered with his team or the NFL—oops. This is why most brands refer to the Super Bowl as "the big game." There is a distinction between the league, the team, and the players, and leveraging all three in a partnership is not only a lot of work but also unaffordable for most brands. That's why athletes often wear generic jerseys in commercials; the colors may match their team's colors, but brands have to pay a separate sponsorship if they want to include the team name or his real number on the jersey.

Our team designed an ad where his face was surrounded by generic clipart versions of his team's logo. It wasn't the official logo, but it created enough of an association to tap into fans' appeal.

There are also stipulations about promoting professional team partnerships outside their designated geographical location. This is why you are unlikely to see commercials, out-of-home advertisements, or social media promotions for teams in different markets. While we know major cities have die-hard fans from other regions, it is ultimately unfair to local markets to allow outside advertisers, even within the same league. It would be similar to bringing your own homemade food to a restaurant. Because you've already spent money making your food at home, you are significantly less likely to spend money on food at the restaurant.

These intricacies are not volunteered or readily disclosed when you engage in sports marketing, whether as a brand advertiser or account manager. This is why I have a deep appreciation for starting my career in sports and marketing early on. On numerous occasions, I've offered cautionary tales derived from my past mistakes, mishaps, or wasted campaign dollars. When you consider the additional complexities associated with alcohol marketing, you might understand why brands actively seek to hire individuals with direct experiences and case studies to offer.

Because the specifics of sports partnership agreements are confidential, there isn't really a way to gauge if a sponsorship deal is comparable to the current market. So unless you have direct experience reviewing sponsorships, there's a chance you're not getting a great deal.

Furthermore, the investments fluctuate based on deliverables and the team's expected performance that season. Fortunately, I can blend my knowledge of investments with long-standing relationships in the industry to gauge whether a sponsorship deal makes sense for a brand. Notably, sports teams typically secure the most sponsorship funding from beverage brands, both alcoholic and non-alcoholic. In a distant second, we find banking and tech platforms, but their investments don't match the scale of those made by alcoholic beverage brands.

I can review a complex, legally worded contract and determine in approximately 10 minutes if the deal is worth the asking price. While you should always have an attorney review any contract you sign, their role is to mitigate liability. However, your job as a brand manager is to pay close attention to what is (or is not) mentioned as an actionable item within the agreement. Far too often, I have seen brands sign deals that do not include social media posts from the sports team's account, assuming it's a given. As is the case with most business agreements, nothing is a given unless it's in writing.

It is also important to note that agreements do not itemize various deliverables by cost. Contract deliverables may include the use of the partnered team's logo, in-stadium advertising, product placement, co-branded campaigns on social media platforms, appearances with certain celebrities or players, meet-and-greets, fan zones, walking on the court or field, tastings, exclusive content, and so forth.

I empathize with smaller, inexperienced brands that blow their entire marketing budget on IP rights, unaware that being the "official" anything of a team is not enough in and of itself. As a brand, it is incumbent upon you to have the marketing dollars—a budget—to activate the IP and build brand awareness. If a tree falls in the forest and no one hears it, did it really fall? No. Similarly, as a brand, if you're the official tequila of a soccer team, and no one knows it, you don't really have a partnership. On top of investing in a sponsorship, brands must build tools and assets that will communicate the sponsorship to your target audience; the sports teams won't do it for you. As brand teams, we build the billboards, hire graphic designers, and do all the heavy lifting to showcase and promote the partnership. Too often, brands and businesses feel good about purchasing a sponsorship, only to lack the budget or strategy to activate it.

Another valuable benefit of sports partnerships is the "first right of refusal." This provision ensures that when a partnership ends, your team partner cannot pursue your competitors for a sponsorship without consulting you first. Having this "first right of refusal" clause is typically advantageous because team partners may possess insights into your business strategies, and you wouldn't want them inadvertently or intentionally sharing that information with your direct competitors in pursuit of a new sponsor. I once found myself in a precarious situation where my team at a whiskey brand terminated a sports partnership, and our direct competitor acquired the partnership and offered me a job to lead the same team and execute similar campaigns.

Another consideration is the strategic utilization of your partner's data to assess consumer preferences, behaviors, and trends, as well as tapping into their email lists to reconnect with the specific audience you're aiming to target.

A recurring challenge in my work is the conflict between the colors of alcohol brands and those of sports teams' uniforms. Given my experience with European vodka, gin, whiskey, and cognac brand teams, I frequently find myself defending the ethos of American football and basketball fans,

"No, Siobhan, Giants fans won't wear green jerseys, no matter how stylish they are."

With over a decade of experience in the sports industry, I am often asked about my favorite team. To put it plainly, I remain neutral about teams, supporting them one season and critiquing them the next. My loyalty ultimately aligns with my paycheck and whoever I am working with in a given season. However, I have but one true favorite—the Alabama Crimson Tide.

My journey to Alabama began when I received a substantial promotion as the state manager of the Alabama and Mississippi markets, managing the marketing efforts for several spirit brands. The cross-country move meant a bigger paycheck and a lower cost of living.

Upon arriving in Alabama, I was essentially a lone employee with significantly stressful responsibilities. It was a challenging period marked by culture shock, long days, and homesickness. Alabama football, however, was a revelation. Unfamiliar with the power of the SEC, I was captivated by the electric atmosphere. Despite my disappointments about life in Alabama, game days became my refuge. Alabama football allowed me to connect with my coworkers, accounts, and neighborhood in special ways.

Beyond this, my career in alcohol marketing has granted me incredible experiences—backstage passes, exclusive dinners, private tours, and even game tunnel access—experiences money truly can't buy. As a beverage partner, you are invited to behind-the-scenes experiences most sports fans could only dream of having! I even received a personal thank-you letter from the Los Angeles Lakers that read, *"You, Ella, were pivotal to our success"* after winning the 2020 Championship Finals. Money cannot buy that.

Some stadium moments are a bit more embarrassing for me, like when I walked through the Hall of Fame suites and spotted a coworker I hadn't seen in a while. I couldn't remember his name, but I approached him anyway, shook his hand, and said, "It's so good to see you here. Have fun. We'll chat soon."

He smiled and said, "Sure thing."

As we walked away, my coworker asked me, "Wait, how do you know Troy Aikman?"

I didn't. I don't. I just thought he looked familiar and said hi. Sometimes, it feels like things like this only happen to me.

Having access to season and suite tickets over the years, I've come across an interesting tidbit about stadiums. Some arenas plant undercover, fake fans in the season ticket sections. These spies wear the away team's gear to spot any season ticket holders behaving badly toward guests. If caught, those ticket holders could lose their season tickets, with no refund. So, if you're going to be a season ticket holder, don't be a jerk—it could cost you.

PART TWO

Tolerance: The act of allowing something.

Usage: *"She had absolutely no tolerance for illegal or immoral behaviors."*

CHAPTER FOUR

For the Culture: The Complexities of Multicultural Marketing

After a year of researching over 40,000 jokes with over two million ratings in 2002, UK psychologist Dr. Richard Wiseman (via The Laugh Lab), proclaimed he'd found the "funniest joke in the world." Here's the joke:

> *Two hunters are out in the woods when one of them collapses. He doesn't seem to be breathing, and his eyes are glazed. The other guy takes out his phone and calls the emergency services. He gasps, "My friend is dead. What can I do?"*
>
> *The operator says, "Calm down. I can help. First, let's make sure he's dead."*
>
> *There's silence, and then a gunshot is heard.*
>
> *Back on the phone, the guy says, "Okay, now what?"*

Did you laugh? Neither did I. While the joke is in no way hilarious, the irony and absurdity of the huntsman scenario are recognizable across multiple languages and cultures, making it the funniest joke in the world.

What I value in this unamusing joke is its ability to illustrate that mass marketing campaigns aimed at a broad audience lack the same depth of emotional connection and impact as tailored or localized marketing efforts. By customizing your brand messaging through channel marketing, customer segmentation, or multicultural marketing, you position your business for significantly higher levels of engagement and conversion rates.

While High Octane is an energy drink known for its trailblazing in the action sports space, the leadership team also started making significant investments in culture (aka multicultural) marketing—a concept that was fairly novel in the 2000s.

My time working for that energy drink gave me the opportunity to understand that multicultural marketing requires a deep understanding of the culture and an authentic voice, which many organizations strive to have today. When executed correctly, multicultural marketing offers a brand an opportunity to connect with consumers in a meaningful way and build strong brand loyalty. Consumers today, especially Gen Z, are acutely aware of brands that authentically engage with their communities, leaving brands in a vulnerable position without the proper teams and agencies to drive relevant conversations and engagements. In other words, it is much harder today for brands to "fake the funk."

With 15 years of experience in social media marketing, I am a digital marketing dinosaur. The first social platform I was slated to engage consumers on was MySpace. Yes, MySpace. #Hashtags were not a common practice or known term. At that time, all digital publicity was good publicity, and the concept of "cancel culture" did not exist. Brands and marketers witnessed a seismic shift thanks to the widespread adoption of the Internet and digital marketing. Through online marketing, we could personalize our brand's narrative and rally support from loyalists.

During this journey, I sometimes leveraged my own presence on social media, shamelessly encouraging consumers to post about their brand experience with me, "Thanks for the Octane, Ella." "Tagging" someone was not yet a concept, so my intention was not to gain "new friends" (today known as followers) but to highlight my work for the brand team at headquarters.

This came to a head when I worked at an event with over 90,000 attendees, sampling High Octanes to the crowd for an entire weekend. As my shift and the evening started to wind down, my backpack was getting light. Here I was, in a crowd of nearly a hundred thousand people, and I only had a few High Octanes samples left. Four guys approached me and asked, "Hey, can we get one?"

I was trying to get away, and I thought, *What am I going to do?*

I was in the middle of a crowd that had been drinking and baking in the sun for hours, and I was by myself. I don't know what came over me, but I crossed my arms, popped my hip, and said, "What are you going to do for it? What are you going to give me?"

They replied, "Well, what do you want?"

"I want you to sing me a song," I teased.

They started laughing, and I thought they would say no, but then they said, "Okay, what do you want to hear?"

"I don't know, there are four of you, so maybe you should sing me Boyz II Men."

Right there on the spot, the guys looked at each other, and, without hesitation, one of them dropped to his knees, and they started singing the ever-romantic ballad, "I'll Make Love to You."

Through their harmonizing, it was evident that they were in some sort of acapella or music group. It was clearly not their first time singing this song. There I stood, being serenaded, as a large crowd gathered around us in awe. Have I mentioned that things like this seem to only happen to me?

Ultimately, I only had *two* Octanes to give to the *four* guys. The crowd went wild, cheering for them and then booing at me. I wanted to run and hide. As I walked back through the hotel lobby at the end of my shift, my boss pulled me aside and said, "Hey, we need to talk. Can you come over here?"

Getting pulled into that hotel conference room for a surprise meeting with high-ups sent a shiver up my spine. I was, once again, convinced I was about to be fired.

The marketing team from HQ and my boss asked, "Do you know why we pulled you in here today?" Word to the wise: Don't answer that question honestly; never guess why; Just play dumb.

So, I said, "No, I'm not really sure what this is about."

They said they wanted to discuss the stunt I had pulled that day. I began shaking. They surprised me by expressing wild interest in my innovation. They explained that, from where they were standing, I had made thousands of impressions on individuals by using just two cans of High Octane. This is when I started learning about the value of cost per impression (CPI) and analyzing returns on marketing investments.

I am unsure why I thought of Boyz II Men when looking at these guys; I could have just as easily asked them to do cartwheels. But in that moment, intentionally or not, I had tapped into a cultural relevance that created a memorable, magical brand moment for hundreds, if not thousands, of people that day.

This illustrates the significance of terms like "reached" and "engagement" when building a brand and cultivating brand loyalists. While our brand *reached* those who walked by or observed, we also *engaged* with the men who were singing and the crowd that responded with cheers (or boos) at the end.

This is extremely relevant in digital marketing; impressions are nice, but engagements, such as a review, a comment, or a share, are better. That day, I concluded that bending the rules was okay as long as the consumer experience was delightful and memorable. Consequently, I became a multicultural lead for the team, occasionally being invited to attend meetings in the headquarters offices to offer ideas or feedback on various campaigns.

Throughout my career, I have used experiences like this to develop and implement culturally relevant programs for some of the world's largest alcohol brands. Thanks to my personal and professional background, I have become a go-to expert for overseeing hundreds of multicultural programs and campaigns across North America, earning numerous accolades along the way.

When discussing multicultural marketing in alcohol brands, multicultural segments are typically divided into Latinx, Af-Am, AAPI, and LGBTQIA+—all of these segments are passion points of mine with personal connections.

Repeatedly, I have surpassed my goals and sales targets by creating incremental business opportunities through various channels, such as e-commerce and multicultural markets.

My strongest passion and emotional connection shine through most prominently in the first multicultural segment, Latinx. This segment holds the closest cultural ties to me, both personally as the daughter of a Mexican immigrant, and professionally, where my budgets have been the highest.

Several jobs I have had throughout the years, starting with High Octane, were contingent on my ability to speak Spanish and build Spanish consumer engagements in an authentic voice, giving me a significant competitive edge. In my observations, very few individuals in the corporate world are fluent in Spanish. How do I know? Because my Spanish is not that great, and I've built a successful career on it. While my mediocre Spanish certainly surpasses my proficiency in, say, Japanese or Italian, it also highlights a significant gap between the Hispanic community and leadership within the corporate beverage industry.

Spending half of my career in California, the lack of *hablantes de español* at my past companies is a bit jarring. Los Angeles, California, has more Mexicans than any other city besides Mexico City. This is likely why some might conflate the terms Hispanic, Mexican, and Latino, even though they are not necessarily interchangeable. Mexican refers to someone from Mexico. Referring to someone as "Hispanic" implies a connection to the Spanish language, excluding Brazilians who speak Portuguese. Similarly, Latino excludes Spain, because it is not in Latin America.

The term Latino might also exclude female Latinas or nonbinary individuals, as it insinuates Latin descent and male gender. This is why the term Latinx was introduced, to include all types of people, encompassing Hispanic, Latino, Mexican, and various cross-segmentations.

The Latinx demographic is exciting to marketers because they have a substantial consumer base in the United States, with rich traditions and diversity. Notably, they have a younger median age in America than any other ethnic group. This presents an exciting opportunity for me as a marketing director in the alcohol space to create campaigns around cultural moments, such as Cinco de Mayo, Día De Los Muertos, Carnaval, and Hispanic Heritage Month. In the early stages of my career, our team distributed items like fake mustaches, sombreros, and maracas, which today could be considered culturally insensitive and tone-deaf. There isn't always room to advocate for better ideas in the multicultural space, especially if you're the only Spanish speaker on a team. This is why I stress the importance of developing Employee-led Resource Groups (ERGs) within organizations to promote cultural competence and provide resources for employees at all levels.

In the alcohol industry, it's interesting that, despite the emphasis on targeting Hispanic or Latinx consumers during cultural moments, there isn't as much representation as expected, particularly at higher-level positions. While you may encounter Hispanic individuals in roles such as warehousing, truck driving, and shelf stocking, there's a notable absence of diversity in directorial and executive positions. From my perspective, when a significant investment of hundreds of millions of dollars is made to target specific populations and encourage increased consumption of alcoholic beverages, a similar level of vigor should be applied to prioritize diverse recruitment efforts.

Another segment close to my heart is Af-Am, short for African American or Black culture. While the industry's desire to target Black consumers has evolved, some marketing efforts remain overlooked, underappreciated, and, at times, offensive due to a corporate misunderstanding of Black consumers and culture.

In my personal life, I strive to move beyond the painful and complicated diaspora history of Black Americans in the United States. However, as a marketer and the daughter of an African-American man, I take historical implications seriously and feel a great sense of responsibility when working on campaigns specifically aimed at Black consumers.

Firstly, history has shown that during the prohibition era, African Americans were disproportionately targeted for liquor-related offenses, considering that slavery had only been abolished 55 years prior. Several decades later, a study from the John Hopkins Bloomberg School of Public Health revealed that in Baltimore, Maryland, Black neighborhoods were eight times more likely to have liquor stores than white or racially integrated neighborhoods.

Often the only Black voice in a room, I have had to carefully navigate extremely uncomfortable conversations behind closed doors regarding what is or isn't appropriate, relevant, or impactful. This is a delicate dance, and sometimes my personal passion shines through, not always resulting in a perfect delivery.

I will never forget firmly saying to a Brand Director, "Don't come to me next quarter asking why we aren't beating other brands in the Black segment," because the brand team refused to publicly or internally address the wake of the BLM protests following the death of George Floyd. Little did that Brand Director know, I was managing backlash from various accounts and sales teams due to the brand's sharp silence.

From my point of view, asking me to develop campaigns and execute advertising targeted at the Black community one month, then staying silent while the world and competitors post in support of Blackout Tuesday the next is contradictory. A few hours later, I received a text from the BD with a screenshot of the brand's statement condemning racism—a little late to the game, but I'll take it.

Personally, I don't believe anyone should feel obligated to post about a particular moment, war, terrorist attack, movement, etc., just because everyone else is doing it. I think society has become overly prescriptive in our expectations of what people should or should not say on their personal social media platforms. However, brands do not have the same privilege of staying silent when faced with uncomfortable issues; as marketers, we need to act swiftly yet authentically. This is why having direct links to the communities you are actively targeting is important.

I am unconvinced that the Af-Am marketing efforts I have put forth have yielded the return on investment that other campaigns have. Black consumers are a complex and nuanced group that several brands fail to communicate with authentically. But despite the possible lack of financial returns, I take tremendous pride in my campaigns in the Black space, where I have been able to highlight and celebrate Black culture, influencers, musicians, business owners, and bartenders in America.

While brands aim for personalized marketing, they have to oversimplify consumer segments, leveraging overbroad data from sources like the Census, Nielsen, IRI, and other market research platforms. One intriguing trend we observe within American retail is that Black consumers exhibit higher purchasing power, even surpassing their Asian counterparts who have higher household incomes (HHI).

Having grown up in an area of Orange County, California, where nearly one-third of the population identifies as Asian-American or Pacific Islander, AAPI, I have witnessed the remarkable intersectionality between Black and Asian cultures in America. It is my observation that brand marketers often overlook the unique blend of Asian and Black influences showcased within basketball, sneaker culture, and rap music. Similar to the Latinx definition, AAPI describes the diverse population of individuals with origins from either the continent of Asia or the Pacific Islands.

Southern California stands out as one of the most culturally diverse regions in the United States, boasting a substantial AAPI population. It is home to a rich tapestry of individuals hailing from East, Southeast, South, and Western Asian regions, making it a true melting pot. Notably, Southern California hosts the world's largest population of Vietnamese people outside of Vietnam's largest city, Ho Chi Minh (formerly known as Saigon). This vibrant blend of cultures creates a dynamic, opportunistic environment for multicultural marketing and engagement.

Although I don't have AAPI heritage, I cherish my childhood experiences within AAPI cultures. I fondly recall my elementary school's Japanese student exchange program, where students from Japan joined our classrooms. They graciously introduced us to various Japanese traditions, such as origami and calligraphy. Memories of Kyoto candy still dance on my taste buds, and I long for the day it will become more affordable and accessible in the States. I also have fond memories of my Indian, Korean, and Filipino classmates sharing their food, holidays, and languages with me.

I deepened my appreciation of Eastern cultures during my undergrad years by taking multiple classes that focused on Asia's business and cultural practices, specifically China, Indonesia, India, and Japan.

Throughout my career, I have encountered challenges in gaining advocacy and understanding of the need for AAPI-centric marketing campaigns. Through case studies, I've highlighted how AAPI consumers wield significant influence and purchasing power in American businesses and culture, as evidenced by the growing popularity of Asian products. Popular grocery chains like Matsuya, a flourishing culinary scene with dishes like pho, ramen, and sushi, influential media trends such as K-pop, anime, and acclaimed productions like *Parasite*, *Squid Game*, and *Bling Empire* serve as excellent illustrations of this phenomenon.

Point blank: If you're a national brand and not positioning yourself for AAPI consumers, then you are not setting your business up for scaling or accelerated growth. I am excited to see more brands positioning themselves for the Asian consumer by investing in relevant influencers, events, and moments, and I take pride in having pioneered various AAPI programming.

Economically, Asian consumers have the highest household income in the United States, making them a key demographic. Again, I must stress that this Asian buyer avatar is monolithic, overbroad, and does not fully grasp the unique, rich experiences of *individuals* within AAPI communities. Nevertheless, I am honored to have been entrusted with the design of campaigns and advertisements that open the gateways to more inclusive marketing efforts.

As a female marketer who has pioneered several LGBT campaigns for alcohol brands, my heart sank when news of the 2023 Bud Light campaign fiasco resulted in severe backlash on the Bud Light brand, the influencer Dylan Mulvaney, and the Anheuser-Busch sales and marketing teams. I don't care to delve too deeply into the details of the campaign's shortcomings and where it went awry. But the ordeal resonated deeply with me for personal reasons. I have a lot of compassion for the precarious situation in which Alissa Heinerscheid, VP of Marketing at Anheuser-Busch, found herself, and I am not entirely convinced she was adequately set up for success. Moreover, it is frightening to imagine that a 48-second video can cost marketing executives their jobs, reputation, and even their careers.

While I can confidently state that such a mess of a campaign would not have happened under my direction or oversight, I also know firsthand that certain marketing tactics are well beyond one person's idea or autonomy. As a marketer in this space, you are put in the awkward and sometimes impossible circumstance of being innovative, trailblazing, culturally attuned, and appealing to fresh audiences without alienating your existing customer base.

Furthermore, the three-tier system outlined in Chapter One makes the business cycle that much more complex. If any tier refuses to purchase or stock your product in the wake of the backlash, your product is dead in the water.

Bearing in mind that when I started in this industry, gay marriage was still illegal in most states, my experiences in LGBT marketing are ones in which I take great pride (no pun intended). However, I have received the most pushback, hesitance, and, frankly, xenophobic comments in response to the work I've been able to do in the LGBT space. The work has been incredibly vibrant and fun in many ways, but in others, my journey has been marked by profound frustration in a quest to maintain advocacy and relevance.

The first time I was hired to activate in LGBT accounts, I was chosen because the predecessor requested not to manage LGBT bars due to personal beliefs. What always bewildered me was that people at the executive level would talk a certain way behind closed doors, but then they were quick to slap a rainbow on their label for public-facing purposes. In my career, I have heard far more homophobic comments than racial or sexual ones, and this has always angered me.

The assumption that I wouldn't have passion or empathy for a group of individuals with whom I don't share specific identities troubles me. I identify with everyone as fellow human beings who share the same desire to be accepted, seen, and loved. I embrace inclusivity not out of convenience or trendiness but because I am a staunch advocate for kindness and fairness for everyone.

So when I was put in the position of working in LGBT accounts, simply because others refused to, I saw it as an honor. Plus, I was super excited and eager to explore different gay bars in Los Angeles and San Diego. These campaigns were bold, vibrant, and we had much more freedom than traditional marketing materials.

To witness and be a part of the radical progress made toward the support and equality of all people within the advertising world has been a remarkable experience. While I am not a member of the LGBT community, I feel grateful and blessed to have been reared as an ally. Despite the array of rainbow vodka bottles produced by conglomerates at one time or another, I believe there is serious work to be done to effectively and authentically appeal to consumers who are so diverse, global, and intersectional in their experiences.

Regarding the four cultural segments mentioned—Latinx, Af-Am, AAPI, and LGBTQIA+—I recognize my limited understanding within each community but strive for cultural awareness, staying attuned to trends, shifts, and shared experiences. Multicultural marketing in the alcohol industry has allowed me to collaborate with diverse thought leaders, enhancing my ability to foster inclusive environments.

In my efforts to make a difference, I've come to the table not believing that I know everything due to my diverse background, but with a determination to highlight and bridge voids where feasible; I'm not sure all leaders approach their work in a similar vein.

I anticipate that as Gen Z enters the workforce, significant shifts will occur, as they are unlikely to tolerate certain diversity issues that have persisted in the alcohol industry for decades. While I'm grateful for certain strides I've witnessed, such as fewer bikini-clad models and increased representation of female executives, we still have a long way to go to create the inclusive, safe, and healthy work environment that everyone deserves.

In the ever-evolving landscape of the beer, wine, and spirits industries, the cry for transparent hiring and promotional practices has never been more resounding. Transparency is the cornerstone of achieving true equity. Without it, the goal of creating an inclusive and diverse workforce remains elusive. It is essential that organizations operating in this space shed light on their hiring and promotional practices to ensure that every individual, irrespective of their background, has a fair shot at success.

For me, one of the more frustrating aspects of climbing through the ranks from the "bottom" as a server and promo model is being privy to the egalitarian mindsets held by leaders who have never worked in the field with us, the common folks. The alcohol industry is built upon the labor of hardworking Americans, including bar managers, liquor store owners, truck drivers, warehouse workers, and vendors. What has made me both unique and successful as a manager, having interviewed and hired hundreds of employees, is my steadfast belief that bartenders and merchandisers are this industry's backbone. They serve as brand advocates and gatekeepers, possessing invaluable customer insights. And yet, you would be hard-pressed to find recruitment efforts aimed at guiding and mentoring top-performing bartenders or merchandisers into full-time sales and marketing positions.

My rallying cry for a more diverse working environment in this antiquated industry does not (just) pertain to one's ethnic or racial background alone. True change comes from nurturing diversity of thought, geographical backgrounds, age, sexual orientations, religious and belief systems, abilities, educational backgrounds, languages, family situations, and working experiences.

I look forward to the day when alcohol suppliers and wholesalers embrace a modern, inclusive environment where every voice is heard and valued at every organizational level.

CHAPTER FIVE

Behind the Spotlight: Celebrities and Influencers

If someone were to ask me, "What are some of the coolest things you've done at work?" I could honestly answer that I've volunteered as a guest bartender at multiple fundraisers, helped a colleague plan his mother's funeral, and provided financial aid to a pregnant coworker navigating divorce. I've also supported my teams in their pursuit of career advancement by reviewing their resumes, redefining their goals, and writing recommendation letters, which ultimately led to many of their promotions. I take great pride in empowering my teams to persevere and strive for personal excellence, and that's pretty cool, if you ask me.

While these actions may sound noble, like something you'd hear at a Miss America pageant, the stone-cold truth is they don't elicit the same level of reactions I get when I say I've bumped into Naomi Campbell, Jennifer Aniston, or Paris Hilton.

The world of celebrities and influencers fascinates me from a psychological standpoint. There is a real power of persuasion at play, a complex phenomenon that impacts our society on both cultural and individual levels. So, whether we like it or not, and whether celebrities like it or not, they do possess a unique ability to shape perceptions and influence behaviors due to their familiarity, strong social standing, and often, great charisma.

When it comes to celebrities, people naturally identify with them, creating a sense of personal connection despite having no real-life interactions at all. By nature, humans desire to associate themselves with high-status individuals, so people will ask celebrities for a photo or autograph. This phenomenon is known as the halo effect, where proximity to someone esteemed can elevate your perceived social status, increasing social recognition and even higher self-esteem.

By utilizing a celebrity endorser, advertisers seek to harness the power of the halo effect, leveraging a celebrity's image to convey that their brand is stylish and appealing. This concept extends even further in the realm of alcohol marketing. For instance, when introducing a new product with uncertain prospects, brands may strategically position their product on the shelf alongside a popular one, signaling to consumers, "Hey, take notice of us; we're next to this guy," even in the absence of an official association.

Celebrities and influencers shape our norms, values, trends, and even policies in America. The Mere-Exposure Effect, developed by 1960s psychologist Robert Zajonc, contends that people tend to trust familiar faces and remember their messages more. Familiarity breeds trust. In fact, even if you don't necessarily like a particular face, you are more likely to trust it simply because it's familiar to you. Brands leverage this trust to endorse their products.

All of this is amplified through social media, given the mass content consumption and short attention spans. Advertising strategies aim to seamlessly integrate their product and brand messaging into channels and content their target consumers already engage with.

Growing up in Southern California, I was exposed to the captivating realm of high-profile living from a young age. The vibrant entertainment industry, inviting weather, and access to luxurious lifestyles made encounters with influential or famous individuals common compared to regions like the Midwest or elsewhere in the world.

My father, a retired LAPD officer, provided firearm consultation for action roles in films and made numerous television appearances. Occasionally, my brother and I had the privilege of joining him on set or in studios, oblivious to the notable individuals around us.

I also graduated from Chapman University, known for its reputable film school. Due to the school's location near entertainment industry centers, it attracted prominent guests, students, or parents of students. My background has given me an unusual opportunity to interact with and get to know eminent individuals in intimate ways.

Though I'm no celebrity or influencer, I've seen the challenges of high visibility. Working for a renowned brand, giving out samples or swag, I've witnessed the public's odd behavior when they act like they know you, but you're a total stranger. Many people approach you and act as if you owe them something. One of the most challenging aspects of working for High Octane was the loss of privacy, especially when we were out and about in the company vehicle. Taking our legally mandated 30-minute lunch break was nearly impossible. Countless times, we threw on unbranded sweatshirts, grabbing a quick meal, only to be interrupted by strangers saying, "Hey, I saw you get out of that car. Can you give me an Octane?" These encounters were sometimes creepy and left us feeling unnerved. Sitting in a parking lot, mapping our route, people would unabashedly tap on our windows or hop on our car, asking for samples. At events, we would get mobbed, pushed, and groped. People would break into our cars. We got called derogatory names. We were expected to address controversies related to the brand that had nothing to do with us as individuals. Folks were relentless and unhinged.

Highways proved to be an arena of uncomfortable attention. People would swerve their cars across lane lines, driving recklessly at 80 mph just to drive up beside us and snap a photo.

I wince when I imagine all the photos taken of me throughout the years, with or without my permission. Thanks to pocket-sized phones with cameras, people can operate as mini paparazzi. Between working at a sports bar, driving the High Octane sports car, and working at hundreds, if not thousands, of sporting, music, and media events, God only knows how many photos of my face are floating throughout the world and the internet. These firsthand experiences of what "fame" feels like are why I would never snap a photo of a famous person without their explicit permission. Having your every move watched and documented by complete strangers is traumatizing.

I can appreciate that people did not see me as Ella Parlor, a student, a daughter, a young woman just doing her job, but as an extension of a beverage they loved. Once we stepped into that car, it was as if we had entered a massive, mobile fishbowl, with all eyes upon us. There was an expectation of being ambassadors of the brand, always looking attractive from every angle. We were expected to drink High Octane at all times—as if humans don't need water, soda, or coffee. We discreetly carried out everyday tasks with our heads on a swivel, whether it was buying a tampon or adjusting our bras because a constant fear lingered that someone might capture an unflattering photo of us. We were sometimes reprimanded if less-than-favorable photos of us were posted online.

But despite these hurdles, high visibility certainly had its perks. In the High Octane sports car, it sometimes felt like we were exempt from traffic laws. If we drove on sidewalks or the beach boardwalk, police officers would laugh and wave as we drove by, probably assuming we had a permit. No parking? No problem. Red zones were like our VIP parking spots because any space felt like it belonged to us in the High Octane automobile. Except for blue handicap-accessible spots—parking in those would be entirely despicable.

Restaurants gave us free food just for parking at their establishments, and gyms gave us free memberships. We were invited to walk at red carpet events. We enjoyed front rows, backstage access, and were snuck into multiple shows. We received personal invitations to the hottest parties in town and to the houses of local athletes and prominent personalities.

For those six to ten hours a day, we were rock stars.

Alas, I was always grateful that I could clock out, take off my uniform, and drive home in my unassuming Scion TC, spending my time off in peace. Recognizable celebrities do not get that luxury. This taste of fame has solidified my belief that being famous is not suitable for someone as sensitive and introspective as I am. Because of my work experiences and outgoing nature, I'm sometimes accused of wanting to be famous, which couldn't be further from the truth. I cherish my anonymity and privacy, and the only name I want people to remember when I die is that of Jesus Christ.

My first few jobs with Tastey's, High Octane, and that ridiculous nightclub prepared me for working with influencers and celebrities on behalf of alcohol brands, where the stakes, visibility, and budgets are much higher.

My first celebrity-facing role in the alcohol space was working at a film premiere sponsored by my favorite rum brand. The job was pretty simple: I had to tell the cast of an extremely popular TV show to walk from point A to point B on the red carpet. I practiced and practiced in my living room, but it was all for nothing because their publicity team did the job for me. I just awkwardly waved as they walked by. "Guess you guys figured it out?" Red carpet events almost always have a liquor sponsor, and throughout my career—which has spanned events in major cities like Los Angeles, New York, Las Vegas, San Francisco, Chicago, and Miami—I've had the unique privilege of sharing fleeting yet memorable moments with various influencers.

A fair warning to my industry friends: I'm about to indulge in some cryptic name-dropping, so if you'd rather skip the cringe, feel free to jump ahead to the next chapter.

From designing a custom bottle that Quavo shared on his Instagram to the lighthearted moment Andy Dick mistook our limo for his and hopped in, my experiences with well-known celebrities have been diverse. A sitcom actor invited my friends and me to his son's 21st birthday, and a Grammy-winning hip-hop artist sent apology flowers for being late to a sponsored event, citing that his mother had taught him better. Sometimes, I'd like to believe that singing with a renowned Houston singer at her Grammy's pre-party is a memory she cherishes as much as I do. There was also the time I was horrified to find out my team had forgotten to stock the backstage bar for a rapper-turned-reality-star before one of his performances. The back bar had only liquor bottles and juice mixers, no cups, and no ice. I ran to the main bar out front and begged for cups, but by the time I got back, he and his crew were already taking swigs straight from the bottles.

At one point, he offered me a drink and said, "What you mix with?"

I softly replied, "Oh, pineapple or cranberry is fine."

He reiterated, "No, what *you* mix with?"

Realizing he wasn't offering to make me a cocktail, I answered, "Oh, Mexican. My mom is Mexican."

He and his crew proceeded to the stage with those bottles in their hand, waving them in the air. There are few things I love more than free product placement.

At a heavy metal festival, I was cautioned that I needed to ensure the headliner stayed away from the alcohol backstage because he had been sober for more than ten years. You could hear a pin drop when we spotted him holding a gin-branded cup by the bar. My heart raced, and I was unsure what to do. "It's just water, everyone. It's just water," he boasted in his British accent. Regrettably and painfully, I have witnessed other celebrities who publicly profess sobriety but succumb to the allure at private soirees.

You, too, could experience backstage access, VIP treatment, and red carpet moments if you enjoy arriving early to set up, enduring sweltering conditions before and after events, working long and unpredictable hours, handling demanding requests, managing high-stress situations, and dealing with challenging personalities. All of this can be yours for the small price of sacrificing weekends, missing important family and friend gatherings, feeling the emotional toll of solo travel, and being unable to share the experiences with loved ones. *Anything* can become routine with repetition, and the novelty is bound to fade.

As I've climbed the career ladder to director-level positions, my interactions with celebrities have noticeably dwindled—life is full of trade-offs that way. In the early years, I grappled with the irony of spending thousands on my corporate Amex card buying drinks and bottle service for clients while struggling to cover my rent. As I ascended in my profession, managing multimillion-dollar budgets, I started to question why I should treat my corporate finances any differently than my personal ones. This revelation prompted a shift in focus, with me placing greater importance on my personal finances and dedicating more evenings and weekends to my loved ones. While the world of entertainment media has been exhilarating, the serenity of privacy has become a treasure I wouldn't trade for the world.

CHAPTER SIX

My Career Cocktail: Strategy and Analytics

"We've seen what you've done, and we want you."

This conversation was straight from my wildest dreams. Here I was, talking to one of the largest alcohol brands in the world, and they "wanted" me. Years of what sometimes felt like clawing my way into meetings, campaigns, and promotions, demanding—indeed, begging—to be heard, seen, and respected, culminated in this single moment. I became a sought-after professional, and my aspirations had materialized: the six-figure job, the company vehicle, the eager assistant, an extensive travel and entertainment budget, and exclusive access to premier events and venues. In many ways, my career has exceeded my expectations and defied the perceptions of those who simply saw me as some bubbly Tastey's or High Octane Girl.

For reasons likely akin to "imposter syndrome," I find myself thrilled about opportunities I've pursued but tend to be cautious when a company pursues me. I surmise that what sets me apart from others is my unusual background in the niche and nuanced segmentation of alcoholic beverages and cultural marketing. **The riches are in the niches.** In the last five years, I've been recruited by and/or interviewed with each of the world's top 5 liquor and beer conglomerates. At one point, I received three job offers in the same week, which, to my surprise, felt more stressful than not having a job. While being pursued for positions is flattering, it remains a source of anxiety for me because, unlike traditional brand marketers who have spent extensive time in academic settings, my career progression has been deeply rooted in real-life field experiences.

Alcohol brands frequently use traditional sales and marketing tools to bolster brand awareness, visibility, engagement, conversion, and advocacy. For those keen on delving deeper into topics like SEO, CRM, digital marketing, and content strategy, a wealth of resources are available in books, online forums, and courses.

In my experience, however, the most impactful campaigns are driven by these standard approaches and under-emphasized strategies such as *mobility, market and data analysis, system operations*, and *personal branding*.

Mobility: In today's globalized business landscape, the adaptability and networking that come with embracing work travel and relocation opportunities hold immense value. Through my experiences, I have built meaningful relationships and adopted best practices from various regions, giving me an unparalleled advantage in my field. I was 19 when I took my first overnight work trip, which required extra office hours and excuse letters for my college professors. Later, I traveled and relocated to several US markets to accelerate my career. These experiences have ingrained in me a recognized philosophy: to grow and evolve, you must be bold enough to step out of your comfort zone. Relocating to various cities on my own, though challenging at times, has shaped my resilience and fostered personal growth. This transformative experience has expanded my horizons, paving the way for even greater opportunities in the future. While I can appreciate the complexities of work-related travel or relocation, especially for those with families, I firmly believe that making such moves in the early stages of your career can lay a solid foundation for future business success. The long-term rewards often outweigh the short-term sacrifices. And if you don't like your new city or office, you always have the option to return home.

Analyzing Market Data: Data analytics and market analysis are about understanding numbers, extracting meaningful narratives, and anticipating future trends. Many view market analysis as tedious, but there's an art to discerning patterns in consumer behavior. Fluctuations in flavor trends, like the surge in watermelon-flavored beverages in 2020 or the citrus dominance in the 2010s, reflect deeper market insights. My role as a marketer is to ensure that innovative products are properly positioned to launch and sell to target markets using consumer data collected from various platforms like online shopping, social media, and panel surveys. While I pride myself on data-driven decision-making and presentations, I find that quantitative data can still be manipulated to tell a particular narrative. This manipulation is exemplified through the mean, median, and mode, which, although based on the exact same data points, can convey very different stories. While data can certainly be skewed by selecting specific time frames, padding the data, or using misleading charts and graphs, I would strongly caution anyone against flat-out fabricating data. I'll never forget when I was sitting in a boardroom with an advertising agency pitching a social media campaign. Their Gen Z observations leaned more toward millennial trends and habits. I understand how older generations might lump these two together, as they share many commonalities. However, where millennials and Gen Zers diverge significantly is in their drinking habits. The agency didn't anticipate that I had recently attended a social media training with a different company just three months prior. So, I inquired about the agency's data source since it directly contradicted my recent learnings.

"Nielsen," they responded quickly.

"Oh, okay. What year? I don't see it listed," I probed further. "Was it a consumer insight or a digital ad study?"

I wasn't trying to scrutinize; I was genuinely curious. There was an awkward shuffling, and it became painfully evident to everyone in the room that the agency had fudged the numbers a bit too much. Even when offering real data, you'll need to back it up when presenting it. So, learn to analyze and extrapolate it as necessary, but never make it up.

System Operations: Marketing doesn't operate in isolation, nor should it. An all-star sales team with an innovative brand marketing team can only go so far if not met with optimal Standard Operating Procedures (SOP). My affinity for system operations, combined with harnessing technology via SaaS platforms, has revealed ingenious solutions in my career. While conducting a training call for a new CRM platform—a fancy way of saying an app that tracks clients and sales—the VP of Operations barked in the middle of my presentation, "Why do I have to be on this call? Who decided we need this tool? Isn't this something—"

I muted him, a capability I don't think he realized was possible, and firmly said, "Frank, the decision to move forward with this sales tracker was not mine. The marketing team is just implementing it. If you have nothing constructive to offer, you can hang up and take your feedback to the CEO."

Frank hung up. The call continued, and he was fired a few months later. Resisting creative, digital solutions or technology is something I never understood. This emphasis on SOP might not possess the glitz and glam typically associated with marketing a new brand, but it is undeniable that operational considerations significantly influence a marketing campaign's success. Often, marketing teams must engage in logistical discussions about a new bottle's design, glass quality, pricing strategies, pallet configurations, freight transfers, and SKU optimization to achieve business objectives.

Personal Branding: Throughout my various roles, my personal brand has remained steadfast over the decades. Those who have worked with me can confidently attest that I operate with integrity, reliability in delivering results, a genuine passion for connecting with people from all walks of life, and a willingness to take innovative risks. Once, while clearing out my mom's garage, I stumbled upon a stack of my high school graduation headshots. On a whim, I stapled them to the back of my business cards as a humorous—yet effective—icebreaker for particularly challenging clients. Although I might not use such an unorthodox approach today, I remain open to ideas, even if they mean risking looking foolish or failing forward.

In 2012, my career took an unexpected turn into consulting when a former colleague, overwhelmed by her new role in a beverage brand, sought my assistance. Gina knew I had previously worked for High Octane and hired me to help her with PowerPoint decks and to speak to retailers about placing the product in their stores. At the time, I was so nervous that my employer would discover my side hustle for another beverage, albeit not a competitor, that I quit after only a few months. That little non-alcoholic brand was eventually sold for billions, with a "B," to a very large beverage company. I still get a twinge of pride when I see that brand on the shelves at just about every retail store in the country.

In 2015, I was again approached by an executive from a brand I had previously worked for, who requested my expertise in developing in-store merchandising assets like shelf talkers, banners, VAP (value-added packaging) gift sets, etc. Once again, nervous about consulting for another brand, I volunteered my time for free and refused any payment. This brand eventually sold for a few million dollars, a figure that, as a humble marketing manager at the time, I considered a bit undervalued for the acquisition. In hindsight, the business owners greatly undervalued themselves, and I believe they could have received a payout nearly ten times higher. Although we all sold ourselves short, I still value the fact that I am keen to say "yes" to opportunities that come my way, even if sometimes reluctantly.

In recent years, as a consultant, I have leveraged my marketing career with major brands to help small business owners drive new business, hone their leadership skills, and craft exit strategies. I've come to believe that soft skills, combined with an authentic drive to help others, are a pivotal counterpart to traditional business methods, especially in the dynamic marketing realm.

PART THREE

Tolerance: A capacity to endure pain or hardship.

Usage: "*Her high tolerance for late nights, early mornings, and demanding clients afforded her a great promotion at work.*"

CHAPTER SEVEN

Stirring Up Success: Leadership Development

"How is it so easy for you to be kind to people, he asked. 'Cause people have not been kind to me." – Rupi Kaur, Milk and Honey

When I was 23 years old, I received an incredible promotion and led my first sales presentation, brimming with confidence and optimism. The marketing programs I presented were built by my predecessor. Though my slides were prepped and ready, my young, fragile emotions were not. With each slide that passed, every point I made, there was a sales rep, hand raised, eager to tell me why it was flawed. Frankly, they ripped my presentation—and, effectively, me—to shreds.

I answered every question with calm resolve and emphasized the sales data behind each proposal. I wrapped up the presentation with my head held high, swiftly packed my laptop, and darted to the bathroom—as fast as my tight pencil skirt would allow—to bawl my eyes out.

I have no shame in admitting that I cry a lot at work, but outside of a major emotional event like a death, I refuse to give anyone the satisfaction of seeing me cry. I usually turn off my camera, run to an empty conference room, or hide in a bathroom stall, just as I used to do in middle school.

Why was I left alone to present to a sales team of men twice my age? Why hadn't anyone warned me that what feels like a fun, awesome idea in the marketing department may, in fact, come across as more work for a sales team? Where was my leadership support? While I've encountered supportive individuals in my career, I have yet to find a guide, a mentor to help me navigate the intricacies of this industry from the inside. My mother often reminds me, "You get to be the change, the leader you never had. That's a beautiful thing!" It's a comforting thought, but sometimes, the weight of being a proactive leader can be heavy.

From my experience, many business classes and training sessions overlook the nuances of emotional intelligence and the importance of leading with honesty and empathy. I strive to be the leader I did not always have.

In 2012, a startling headline from Forbes caught my eye: "The Majority of Americans Would Rather Fire Their Bosses than Get a Raise." The article delved into a surprising statistic: a staggering 65% of Americans would choose a new boss over a pay increase. The timing was uncanny. That same month, I stepped into the manager role for the first time.

My promotion wasn't the result of some leadership epiphany; it was circumstantial. I had excelled in my previous position, and when my manager unexpectedly left, I was the logical replacement. In many corporations, it's commonplace to promote high-performing individuals based on their current skills rather than preparing them adequately for their new roles. Confronted by the weight of managing over 100 part-time employees and the reality of that Forbes article, I had a sobering realization: **what made you successful today might not be enough to**

make you successful tomorrow. Sure, I was great at sales, reporting, merchandising, and relationship building as a promo model, but was I equipped for the myriad responsibilities that came with managing a full-fledged team?

Recognizing the importance of effective leadership, I was motivated to hone my management skills and discovered Jill Geisler's book, *Work Happy: What Great Bosses Know*. Her insights resonated deeply with me, especially as I was determined to be an effective leader. Effective leadership, to me, goes beyond driving marketing campaigns or achieving sales targets and lies in fostering soft skills like open communication, building trust, navigating conflicts, and stimulating creativity. In light of the 2020 global pandemic, which underscored the importance of employee well-being, job satisfaction, and workplace morale, I anticipate more companies will be forced to recognize and prioritize these *softer* aspects of leadership.

Today, my passion for mentoring, guiding, and collaborating with professionals stems from my experiences with both exceptional and challenging bosses. Each has imparted invaluable lessons that shape my approach as I lead and coach individuals in the workplace.

During my tenure as a cashier at Vita Vibe, I encountered a pivotal moment that would shape my approach to leadership. When my boss castigated me in front of customers, I mustered the courage to address the situation directly in her office. Borrowing a cue from Terrence Howard's character in the movie *Crash*, I bemoaned, "You embarrassed me. You embarrassed yourself." This confrontation was my first time managing up, and to my surprise, it culminated in a genuine apology. Not only did I demonstrate that leadership is not confined to titles, but my boss also exemplified that true leadership is defined by actions, empathy, and a readiness to reconcile.

As leaders, we ought to appreciate the tremendous bravery it takes for an employee to express that his or her needs are not being met. While being called out never feels good, it's an invitation to stop doing harm and make amends. If we don't challenge each other to be better, how can we expect to develop into better leaders ourselves?

I was confronted in a similar fashion when a top performer shared his concerns with me about a team icebreaker question that I had used for years.

"Ella," Kevin said firmly, "by asking me who my celebrity crush is, you're putting me in a position to either announce my status as a gay man or lie and pretend I'm interested in women, which makes me uncomfortable."

My icebreaker question, "Who's your celebrity crush?" had always seemed innocent enough to me, a heterosexual woman who doesn't have to worry about the implications of answering, "Michael B. Jordan, Wakanda forever!"

Kevin's feedback was enlightening—sometimes, my intentions do not always outweigh the impact of my words. As leaders, it is crucial to cultivate a safe, trusting environment where team members can offer candid insights. I was grateful to Kevin for his candor and for teaching me a new perspective; most notably, I offered him a heartfelt apology and made changes to our new-hire icebreaker questions.

Throughout my career, I have observed that although acknowledging mistakes and shortcomings could prevent significant conflicts or blowback, genuine apologies from leadership teams remain rare. Therefore, I strive to offer a radical counterbalance by leading with the authenticity, vulnerability, and transparency I would have wanted from my past leaders, which includes being quick to apologize. When the need arises, I prioritize face-to-face or verbal apologies, then echo my sincere apology in writing so they can re-read it later or forward it as they see fit. (I can hear my previous HR managers clutching their pearls now.) Such openness may seem unconventional, especially in an antiquated industry like alcohol, but I believe in standing by my words and seeking ways to improve. Although apologies can be seen as admissions of guilt, potentially leading to legal issues, I wonder how many blowouts and lawsuits might have been avoided if people in leadership positions had simply apologized.

One evening, before an activation around the Grammy Awards, I spotted a VP of a tequila brand I was working for at the time in my hotel lobby. He was my boss's boss's boss. I was confident he had no idea who I was but wanted to introduce myself.

"Hi, I'm Ella," I said, casually keeping my association with the brand under wraps to avoid admitting I had already stalked him on Google and LinkedIn. Before I could feign surprise about being in town for the same reason and working for the same company, the conversation took a dark turn. My size 11 feet and high heels became an unexpected and unsettling focus as he made a sexual proposition about them. I was mortified for several reasons: I've always been self-conscious about my large feet; he was clearly oblivious to the fact we worked for the same company and I was in a serious relationship. Afraid of offending him, I excused myself, scurried up to my hotel room, and called my mother, who reassured me he was probably drunk and would forget the encounter by morning.

His cold, furious stare at our team breakfast the next day suggested otherwise. It felt as if he blamed me for some perceived deceit, as if I had enticed him to profess his kinky foot fetish. Intimidated, I did my best to steer clear of him, but as a powerful VP, he oversaw all the programs and work my team did. He repeatedly thwarted my attempts at career advancement.

The first time it happened, I'd already signed an offer letter for a promotion to our Chicago office, where he was based. He urged the brand director to rescind the offer. The hiring manager shrugged, "He said that you're still needed in SoCal. You should be flattered that he knows your work."

"Who revokes an offer after it's been set in ink? What makes him think I won't quit on the spot?" I scoffed at my boss. While I suspected he harbored resentment from the embarrassment of our initial encounter, I clung to my mother's advice that, as a powerful man, he probably didn't remember me and just had someone else he wanted for the Chicago-based role.

The apex of tension arose when I petitioned for a different promotion and a raise, which my boss approved but was denied by the same VP. Livid and painfully aware of this pattern, I called his line directly, completely ignoring the hierarchical chain of command.

"Why do you keep intercepting my attempts at upward mobility in this company?" I asked firmly and frankly when he answered my call.

"Well, Ella, we have never had a Brand Director under the age of 30—can you imagine the optics?"

That was the first time I had ever heard "optics" used outside of the context of eyeglasses. Aware that referencing age as a factor in hiring decisions was illegal, I decided to negotiate for the first time in my career. I proposed that if optics were the concern, I'd stay in my role provided I received a $30,000 raise.

"Thirty thousand dollars, Ella? You can go fuck yourself with that one."

Remembering his words today still brings a fire to my belly. Blind with rage, I made a promise.

"If I walk, you will have to pay two people to replace me," I muttered through my clenched teeth.

Never one to make idle threats, I resigned within four weeks and joined another big industry player. Six months after my departure, validation came when I was informed that my successor was unable to oversee the team, program, analytics, insights, and key account relationships I had once managed. My former boss needed to hire a second person and asked if I'd consider returning. Flattered and vindicated, I smirked from my new office and said, "No thanks, I am really happy here."

As frustrating as that entire experience was, I now reflect on it with a sense of pride. It was a pivotal moment when I recognized my worth and defended it. And when he tried to demean me, I transformed his dismissive remarks into rocket fuel for my career advancement. Today, whenever doubt or intimidation creeps in, I replay that VP's words in my head for motivation, "You can go fuck yourself."

For a while, I pondered whether he had held a personal grudge against me or if I was just overthinking it. Then, as fate would have it, I bumped into that VP in Las Vegas. The encounter was lighthearted and nostalgic as we made small talk about my new job. Before parting ways, he came up close to my ear and whispered that he fondly recalled the night we first met, even mentioning the peep toe of my heels. He had remembered the hotel lobby evening all along—I knew it!

Looking back, the situation might read like a textbook case of sexual harassment: an exec behaves inappropriately, the employee rebuffs him, and he retaliates by obstructing her advancement. However, in the midst of it, things felt unclear and uncomfortable. Without a coach or mentor to validate my experiences, I accepted that this is how the "real world" works sometimes. Dwarfed by his authority, I never had the nerve to confront him and instead worked harder to appease him. While I felt his remarks were overtly sexual and inappropriate, they weren't intended to create a hostile working environment; he didn't even realize I worked for his team when we met. I can't help but wonder how the situation might have shifted if he had just set aside his embarrassment and fear and apologized like an adult. Even if I could prove he was obstructing my career path intentionally, I would have never complained about it formally anyway.

In any sector, coming forward with a sexual harassment complaint is fraught with complexities. But in the alcohol industry, it feels like a professional death sentence. With his charisma, good looks, and oversight of what I estimate to be over $300 million in annual sales, this VP seemed untouchable. From my observations, even after the #MeToo movement, allegations of impropriety often lead to victim-blaming and mistrust. Unfortunately, many speak up only after being laid off or fired, timing that can portray them as merely disgruntled employees.

I have a tremendous amount of respect for the valiant women and men who've spoken up against harassment. Despite stomaching inappropriate comments, advances, jokes, touching, fondling, texts, and retaliation, I have never had the courage to share that part of my story openly. And I have yet to witness a sexual harassment claim being treated with the gravity it deserves. My hope has always been to drive meaningful change from a leadership position, but I'm also willing to admit that this logic is flawed and only perpetuates the hushed conversations around sexual harassment, which remains a prevalent concern in this industry today.

As a manager who has fielded countless complaints, ranging from harassment to retaliation to favoritism, I have observed that HR's role is to protect the company, not the employees. I've gently cautioned others that going to Human Resources may paint the employee as a potential threat or liability. As a people leader and manager, I have also been the subject of numerous complaints about performance evaluations, favoritism, and unfair treatment. Candidly, every time an employee has approached HR or my superior without discussing their concerns with me directly, HR supported me. Why? More often than not, I've been able to predict when a complaint might arise, typically in response to addressing an individual's underperformance.

Additionally, I maintain comprehensive records of professional interactions that strike me as unusual or concerning. To this day, I have yet to receive any formal reprimands for complaints filed against me. Take from that what you will. The established chain of command is there for a reason, and attempts to bypass it—be it through sneaky blind copy email tactics or directly approaching higher-ups—might backfire. At times, HR has even suggested I put the complaining employee on a Performance Improvement Plan (PIP) as a potential precursor to phasing them out.

This underscores why I urge my team to communicate their concerns directly with me or their immediate supervisor before escalating an issue to develop a positive path forward together. While I am far from a perfect boss, my top priority is fostering a safe and inclusive workspace where everyone can collaborate effectively. This commitment is demonstrated by the fact that I continue to invest in my personal growth by reading books, taking online courses, attending training sessions, and engaging in sensitivity sessions to enhance my leadership skills.

Employees sometimes lack a broader view of workplace dynamics, such as relationship nuances or unspoken politics to which they may not be privy. I genuinely wish more employees recognized the strategic advantage of supporting their bosses. While it might seem that a superior takes undue credit, they could also shield their teams from undue blame. Elevating your boss can cultivate a bond, a mentorship, and a mutually beneficial partnership.

Instead of harboring resentment or wanting their bosses to be fired, I'd love for employees to channel their energy into personal growth and networking. While dealing with a difficult boss is challenging, navigating difficult or quirky personalities only intensifies as you climb the corporate ladder. Consider, for instance, CEOs. They may appear omnipotent, but they are beholden to stakeholders, board members, investors, clients, legal entities, the media, and their industry peers. Sometimes, CEOs serve as scapegoats, falling on swords to protect the company's image. **In business, everyone is held accountable to someone.**

These kinds of insights are not always shared openly, which is why it is crucial to seek out a mentor at any organization in which you hope to progress. If a mentor at work eludes you, consider leveraging a strategy that high-performers use: consistently investing in coaching and mentorship to reach accelerated growth and success. I would not have the career I have today if certain individuals had not guided, encouraged, and challenged me to search for answers and solutions within myself, including my own career coach, Farah Bernier.

A leadership role often brings with it an unanticipated sense of isolation, especially when faced with challenging decisions. I first turned to a career coach when I was asked to list which members of my sales support team would face an impending layoff. While I've never initiated a layoff, having to single out individuals has always been profoundly difficult. My colleagues are more than just names in an email; they're individuals with mortgages, families, and aspirations. I believe that while unpopular decisions must be made, humanity mustn't be lost in the process.

I've experienced both sides of layoffs — being part of them and being affected by them. Being laid off feels like a public breakup, with the added stress of financial uncertainty. I know firsthand that after a layoff, the silence from colleagues can be piercing. I imagine many fear saying the wrong thing, but I would argue that reaching out, offering a kind word, or perhaps a LinkedIn recommendation could make a big difference in someone's world during a layoff. I find it best to say, "You've done great work before, and you will do great work again," pointing out their past wins and future potential.

I am far from a perfect boss, colleague, or mentor, but I have always aimed to offer my team more than just sales quotas. Beyond selling alcoholic beverages, my true passion lies in helping others achieve their personal and professional dreams. I firmly believe that to be truly impactful leaders, it's crucial to prioritize continuous development and growth. By doing so, we can effectively guide and inspire our teams, illuminating the path to success in their careers.

CHAPTER EIGHT

Uncomfortably Numb: The Darker Side of Alcohol

"You saved my life, you know," mumbled a man in a tattered jean jacket. He spoke under his breath while sitting alone. Though his eyes stared straight toward the bar, never veering in my direction, his heavy silence suggested he was speaking to me. His hands were weathered and leathery, marked with scars and scabs. As he took another sip of his neat whiskey, I noticed black soot under his fingernails.

I love a good dive bar. There's something genuine about a place where you can just be yourself and chat with everyday folks—the salt of the earth. Sure, you might run into a rowdy character occasionally, but that's half the fun. I've partied in some of the world's top clubs, from LA to Miami to Europe, sharing oxygen with stars like Drake and Tiësto. But honestly? I'd choose a laid-back evening by a broken jukebox over a flashy club any day.

"Who saved your life? And what is that yucky swill you're drinking?" I joshed in my typical irreverent fashion. "You know what? I'm about to upgrade you to some real whiskey."

"No," he contended, taking another swig and turning his head in my direction. "You did. You saved my life." His eyes met mine for a brief second before returning his gaze to the bar in front of us.

"Not you," he admitted softly. "Someone like you. A liquor rep."

Oh, great. I thought. My marketing compliance courses have taught me that when someone conflates enjoyment of alcohol with feeling better or "saving their life," we should try to disengage and prevent irresponsible drinking.

"I mean it," he continued while pulling out a crushed pack of cigarettes from his jacket's front pocket. "You have no idea the impact you have on people by doing your job."

He then asked me to join him outside for a cigarette break as he outlined the night he had intended to take his own life.

One evening several years ago, Wade had lost his job, his dog, and his mom in the same week. Disinterested in seeing what his future had to offer, he decided to end his life. In an attempt to enjoy one final hurrah, he visited his favorite bar to get some liquid courage.

This, unfortunately, is a commonality with suicide. According to several studies, alcohol is involved in anywhere from 25% to over 75% of deaths by suicide in the U.S. This is exacerbated by the fact that heavy drinkers are more likely to take their own lives than their sober counterparts. But as Wade closed his tab, about to head home and end it all, a beautiful promo model holding a tray of some type of liquor samples approached him with the biggest smile and asked if he wanted a "free shot." Again, the alcohol marketing compliance in me would like to clarify that the shot was likely a legally sized half-ounce sample, not a full shot. But I digress.

Wade explained that instead of going home, he sat and chatted with the promo model for about 30 minutes.

"She saved my life just by talking to me and reminding me that the world isn't so bad at all, and you will never know how many times you've touched people in the same way." Wade firmly planted his cigarette butt in an ashtray and nudged us to go back inside.

I was at a loss for words, but I deeply appreciated him sharing such an intimate story. I expressed my heartfelt sorrow for his profound losses and conveyed my gratitude that fate allowed our paths to cross. The night I met Wade in a quiet dive bar in San Bernardino, California, is seared into my memory.

During that period, I also worked as a promotional model, distributing "free shots" to hundreds, and sometimes even thousands of people, several times a week. I felt confined by my role, reduced to just a cute face in a tight dress, knowing my potential and career aspirations stretched beyond that. My feelings, like my cocktails, are often mixed when I reflect on my career. I wear my achievements with pride, having broken barriers and curated amazing experiences for countless individuals. Yet, I can't help but grapple with the rising trend of alcohol consumption in our nation and the extent of responsibility I bear for it. The irony is not lost on me as we slap "drink responsibly" on each bottle in the name of corporate social responsibility (CSR).

In conjunction with our external campaigns encouraging moderation, internal marketing experts in the alcohol space are subjected to monthly training seminars and meetings to stay abreast of market trends, liquor laws, and various liabilities. And because we face serious sanctions, infractions, and fines if we break the law, we require extreme sensitivity to noncompliant or concerning practices.

Both ethically and financially, it's in our best interest that only adults of legal age consume our products responsibly, including ourselves. A common misconception about our work environment is that we're a group of reckless party animals forcing drinks upon our customers to boost sales. This isn't entirely true. After all, the first rule of being a drug dealer is that you can't get high off your own supply. Several of us in the industry, though not me, remain completely sober and abstain from alcohol.

We are subjected to random drug tests, undergo intensive background checks, and if you've ever been arrested for a DUI, your career here is essentially over. I would even venture to guess that you might find more alcoholic lawyers, nurses, or police officers than in our line of work because an alcoholic in our business poses a significant liability. Can you imagine the headlines? *"Booze Exec's DUI takes innocent lives."* The media would have a field day, and no brand could recover from the backlash, the lawsuits, and the fines.

While many might assume alcoholism is more rampant here, I'd argue the opposite. In our industry, the constant proximity to alcohol means that it becomes evident much faster if someone has a drinking problem.

Consider, for instance, our corporate offices. In the same way Nike's headquarters have sporting facilities and display shoes in common work areas, we proudly decorate our walls with liquor and employ full-time bartenders. It wouldn't raise an eyebrow if I contacted our in-house mixologist about an upcoming ad campaign or photoshoot, requesting a unique vodka martini twist at 10:00 a.m. It would also be perfectly normal to taste the martini and invite others passing by the office to sample it with me. However, more often than not, we simply discard the entire cocktail because we have more pressing work awaiting us in our cubicles. I am not an expert on alcoholism, but my understanding is that alcoholics struggle to moderate their alcohol consumption.

Given the easy access to liquor, corporate Uber accounts, and invitations to the hottest spots in town, it's not hard to imagine how someone might become more vulnerable to alcohol overindulgence. The nature of this industry makes it quite easy to identify someone battling alcohol dependency. There have been times when I've pulled teammates aside to firmly advise them to address their drinking problem or consider leaving their job. Some heeded my warning and found a new path, but unfortunately, others met their professional downfall.

I can't help but notice the overwhelming presence of alcohol-related themes in everyday culture. A quick browse on popular online shops like Etsy and Amazon brings up a plethora of alcohol-themed products, including wine sippy cups for toddlers. Although alcohol suppliers don't produce these items, they do violate CSR guidelines.

This probably contributes to my discomfort with the "mommy juice" trends and jokes. Making light of "mommy flasks" and "dads and grads" celebrations worries me because it insinuates that parents, especially mothers, need alcohol to handle life's challenges. The trend is so widespread that I see moms on platforms like TikTok creatively concealing wine in their kids' drink pouches—even though drinking in public is illegal. This blending of parenting and alcohol as a joke feels like it's veering dangerously close to trivializing a more significant issue.

When you take a break from drinking, whether for a brief cleanse, pregnancy, or personal reasons, the omnipresence of alcohol becomes more conspicuous. From hair and nail salons to retail shopping—alcohol is strategically offered to enhance customer experiences and encourage more spending. Celebrations involving children, such as baby showers, gender reveals, or even first birthday parties, are sparkling with champagne and seltzers. Can we no longer enjoy and celebrate the children in our lives without a buzz?

I find this insidious normalization, masked by humor, particularly worrisome. Our culture is becoming irreverent and flippant, inserting alcohol into places where, I believe, it does not belong. Recently, I attended a Namaste Cabernet class with friends, where we were served wine after our yoga session. While I was in Savasana, trying to find inner harmony, my meditation was interrupted by explanations about the types of wine we were going to have. This felt strange and sacrilegious.

I've built a career around promoting alcohol, so I am hardly one to preach total abstinence. However, as alcohol becomes increasingly integrated into our daily lives, it's important to consider how it might be blurring boundaries and diluting our human experiences.

I might be a bit sensitive, but it strikes me as curious that Congresswoman AOC, with her relatable background as a bartender, chose to kickstart her presence on Threads—a new social platform rivaling Twitter—with content related to cocktails. This situation becomes intriguing when you consider her "Cocktails of the Revolution" initiative, especially because her home state of New York is where multiple alcohol corporations have their headquarters. Although she is undoubtedly one of the most likable politicians with a significant social media presence and a devoted following, it's important to address the ethical concerns when a public figure uses her influence to promote alcohol consumption. This is especially concerning because there is a well-documented link between alcoholism and homelessness, which is a pressing issue in her own District.

Reiterating my nonpartisan stance, as mentioned in Chapter One, I believe that a population dealing with alcohol dependence could potentially contribute significant tax revenue to our government. However, I acknowledge that this viewpoint might be a bit of a stretch.

Considering my career path, I am acutely aware of the striking hypocrisy in my observations. It's only recently that I've chosen to address the widespread issue of alcoholism and reflect on my role in perpetuating it.

"We need to find ways to engage consumers when they are at home relaxing," an SVP proclaimed in a meeting. *Wait, what?* I thought to myself, *Are we trying to market alcohol as a relaxation tool? Doesn't that violate our CSR?* I have always understood that solitary drinking could exacerbate isolation and loneliness, potentially leading to addiction or other mental health disorders. My skin was crawling as visions of my boyfriend passed out on his sofa popped into my head.

I first met Ales on a warm summer Texas evening at a sports bar, where we argued about our favorite college basketball teams. We spent months as platonic friends, exploring the city and swapping life stories. Our outings included champagne brunches, football tailgates, and lively parties where the air was filled with our laughter and the melodious clinking of glasses.

As our friendship grew, it became clear there was something more between us, and we shared a whiskey-stained kiss on a Dallas rooftop. Looking back, our relationship's beginning marked its conclusion.

Transitioning out of the honeymoon phase and prioritizing my health, I stopped drinking and devoted more weekends to working out instead of our usual excursions. My decision to abstain from drinking had two main motivations: I wanted to lose weight, and I wanted to encourage, or perhaps inspire, Ales to drink less—you know, the idea of "monkey see, monkey do"? My sobriety began to cast a harsh spotlight on his inebriation: the crimson flush of his face, the slight cross of his eyes, the slurred words, and his tendency for loud outbursts. In an effort to reduce his alcohol intake, I poured his Old Fashioneds with a bit less whiskey. I strategically moved his cocktails around the kitchen, preventing him from mindlessly sipping them while we discussed current news or events.

"You're no fun when you don't drink," he'd blurt out. "I don't understand why you stopped drinking. Isn't that bad for business, Ella?" He was mocking my lifestyle and profession in one sweep.

What does my job have to do with this? I wondered.

In my line of work, if someone declines a drink, we don't pressure them. As sales and marketing professionals, we respect that drinking is an adult's personal choice. If they decide to drink, we want it to be one of our brands, but we respect one's choice to abstain for any reason. I realized that *my* not drinking highlighted how much *he* was drinking for both of us. It became clear that I couldn't possibly ask him to stop drinking while enthusiastically celebrating the success of a gin brand I was actively developing—the contradiction was too stark to reconcile.

For years, I had made a fabulous living convincing adults to purchase alcoholic cocktails, gift packs, glassware, and merchandise I had designed. But now, I found myself unsure how to ask someone I love to stop.

Of all the alcohol sales and marketing meetings I have attended over the past decade, none have offered advice on how to address concerns about excessive drinking in our personal lives, not even once.

Confronting someone about their drinking is unsettling because it often triggers denial, fear of judgment, guilt, shame, loss of control, and defensiveness. I would argue that the impending discomfort leads many of us to silently watch our loved ones succumb to a booze-fueled demise, hesitant to intervene.

The tipping point for me arrived during a somber evening at a restaurant. My seat was pressed against the wall, offering me a view of the entire establishment. I gently expressed that my feelings were hurt over something Ales had said a few nights prior. Defensive, he retorted in a thunderous voice, "You're lying. You're making this up just to make me feel bad," oblivious to the fact that the entire restaurant, including the staff, had turned to stare at us.

Once again, unbeknownst to him, I had ordered mocktails while he sipped on Old Fashioneds. As he raised his voice, visions of my unborn children sat behind him, their legs swinging in the air as they watched this man publicly berate and humiliate me—*not my kids, not my husband*. Vowing that it would be the last time he yelled at me, I ended the relationship with a heavy, broken heart.

In past breakups, I had leaned on drinking to numb the rawness of my emotions, uttering phrases like, "I'm single now. [Take a shot.]" "Forget him. [Take a shot.]" "I'm conquering my pain—I deserve this. [Take a shot.]" But this time, I had already embarked on a journey of sobriety. I was not going to allow a breakup, instigated by someone else's struggles with alcohol, to disrupt my sobriety cleanse.

It struck me that this was the first breakup I had ever navigated with complete clarity. In the past, my demanding career provided both distractions and justifications for me to drink after a breakup whenever I felt the need to do so. This proved to be the most excruciating breakup I had ever experienced, and I was forced to bear my pain without the solace of alcohol. I wept until I vomited, unable to focus on my job. I realized that I had never faced such a challenge without alcohol's crutch, and it hit me hard. In the depths of this unexpected sober breakup, I unearthed a transformative strength I would soon need again.

PART FOUR

Tolerance: a sympathy for beliefs or practices differing from one's own.

Usage: *"The transformation of her beliefs forced her to practice tolerance toward her own evolution."*

CHAPTER NINE

A Sobering Epiphany

October is my favorite month. You get the fall weather, football tailgates, Halloween, football homecoming games, pumpkin spice-flavored everything, and did I mention football? It also happens to be my birthday month, which I have celebrated shamelessly and vivaciously for as long as I can remember. And as dramatic as it sounds, in October 2022, my life changed forever.

"I don't have time for this. We're not even in the playoffs yet, and my birthday is next week. Can we just wait until March after the Super Bowl is over?" I asked my doctor with the utmost sincerity.

"No, you don't have until March," she retorted.

"I don't have until March? That sounds dramatic." I said, unaffected.

"Ella, the tumor you have is the size of a grapefruit."

I thought, *Grapefruit? Big whoop.* By the ripe age of 32, I have had more cysts, tumors, and surgeries than anyone else my age that I know. The first lump I found was when I was nine years old, playing hide-and-seek, crouched in my closet. As I tucked my knees close to my chest, I felt an "owie" and noticed a lump. My mother took me to the doctor, who assured us that it was likely caused by pre-pubescent hormones and that the lump (probably a cyst) would disappear with age, and it did.

Thereafter, I've frequently visited hospitals and treatment centers, often taking time off work for appointments and procedures. Although I've never received a cancer diagnosis, my complex medical history has made me an oncological patient, a fact I've largely kept private for decades.

Since I was fifteen years old, my physical health has followed a pattern: I start feeling unwell but keep it to myself, my condition worsens, I eventually visit a doctor, receive recommendations which I often disregard, my condition deteriorates further, I return to the doctor, finally get treatment, experience relief for a few years, and then the cycle repeats itself. Over the years, I've undergone an excessive number of medical procedures and radiation, including X-rays, CT scans, MRIs, iodine therapy, and radiology, far more than anyone should in their lifetime. My father, who has reservations about Western medicine, once posed a thought-provoking question: "At what point does the cure become the cause?" It's a sentiment I share.

At the age of fifteen, I received the disheartening news that my prospects of having children would be more challenging compared to other women. This was due to my severe endometriosis, a condition characterized by the formation of blood clots and cysts on my reproductive organs, and sometimes even affecting my spleen, bladder, and stomach. Most individuals with endometrial diagnoses like mine can lead relatively normal lives despite enduring substantial physical pain, financial burdens, and emotional strain. My situation, however, is further complicated by severe anemia, temporary hemophilia type II, and an as-yet unidentified tendency for my body to develop tumors on major arteries and blood vessels.

One thing I have always appreciated about the cold, clinical manner in which medical professionals speak is their artful nonchalance. They can casually claim, "Don't worry; this is not cancer or anything," reassuring us of any concerns or bad ideas Google or WebMD might have placed in our heads. I have only had a handful of experiences where a specialist has told me they are concerned and escalated me to a different specialist.

I am no stranger to cancer scares, but I'd be lying if I didn't admit to losing sleep with every single one. In those moments where I have had to contemplate my mortality, I have always found solace in knowing that while I have not lived a full life, I have always lived my life to the fullest.

My medical history pains me spiritually, emotionally, financially, and physically—and it is certainly not sexy. My conditions have impacted my personal life in intimate, humiliating ways. I imagine this is why I have always found reprieve in pouring myself into my school and professional work. I use my fear, my anger, and the realization that I will die to drive myself to do the most and do my best every day.

"Ella, the tumor you have is the size of a grapefruit, and your uterus is the size of your fist. Do you understand?"

Grapefruit, huh? I could really use a fresh Paloma right now.

As I mentioned in the opening chapter of this book, I am not a doctor, but I did major in Pre-Med Biochemistry in college for a solid semester or two before dropping out to study Strategic Communications instead. Also, having spent a large chunk of my life speaking to medical professionals, I know that physicians like to prescribe, pathologists like to test, and surgeons like to cut. Most doctors are going to recommend the treatment route within their specialty because that's what they know best. So, when my brilliant surgeon told me I needed surgery immediately, I was suspicious.

"Well, Doc, babies grow to be the size of watermelons, which are bigger than grapefruit. Do you understand?" I affirmed confidently.

My doctor responded slowly, "Uh-huh... but Ella, you're not pregnant, which means you don't have the hormones to stretch your uterus. It's about to rupture."

Rupture? Oh, fuck. I do not like the sound of that at all. If your uterus ruptures, there is not only a risk of death, but also the inability to have biological children.

"I don't know, doc. Maybe I should freeze my eggs or something before we start cutting into my baby-maker parts."

She let out a disappointed sigh, "Ella, I am also a fertility surgeon. If you want to discuss fertility treatments when you wake up from your surgery, I will do that with you. Freezing your eggs isn't something you can do overnight; it takes months of hormones and harvesting. Your eggs won't mean anything to your family if you're not here."

"Doc, that's like the third time you've insinuated I could die or something," I stammered.

Cue really awkward silence and stern look.

"Like I said, we have grave concerns and need to take immediate action."

And just like that, my days of whirlwind meetings, travel, negotiations, and high-stakes decisions were put on hold as I took medical leave from work. When your life (or your ability to make life) is at risk, the world stops—nothing else matters. My perspective shifted immediately.

Yes, I have an extraordinary career of which I am incredibly proud, but my ultimate desire has always been to have a family. During job interviews, when faced with the absurd question, "Where do you see yourself in five years?" my response has remained consistent. I inquire if they want my honest answer or the polished one. Thankfully, everyone picks the honest one because I don't have a polished answer. I then explain that despite being single with no children (at the moment), I intend to start a family within the next five years, and I view this job as a stepping stone to help me achieve that goal.

Here I was, at 33 years old, seemingly at the pinnacle of what feels like an incredible career. While many women my age are busy popping out their third or fourth kid and hosting yet another gender reveal, I had an engorged belly with a tumor inside my baby chamber—*oh, fate, you cruel and spiteful bitch!*

Although I was living in Texas at the time, I booked a one-way flight home to Southern California because I knew I could not go through the recovery alone. I was also unimpressed and concerned when my Texas doctor, who found the tumor, suggested I have a full hysterectomy and expressed that I should just be grateful I wasn't pregnant because "we'd have to terminate it." With that heartwarming silver lining, I knew it was time to head home to the team of doctors who had treated me before and were familiar with my history and background.

A myriad of complications and concerns regarding my risks of bleeding out, possible cancer, and insurance coverage made my eligibility for surgery a bit convoluted. Spiritually, I have always been comfortable praying for others or myself, but for the first time in my life, I was so desperate I started asking my friends to pray for me and pray hard. I did not give specifics, just that the stressors of my life needed to be alleviated and that I was really scared. Churches, prayer groups, Bible studies, family, and friends around the world had my back. As a Catholic Christian, I have always known deep in my heart that miracles happen daily, but I never imagined I would be worthy of one, let alone multiple. But with every plea and prayer, another miracle occurred, opening the next door to get me into surgery as soon and as safely as possible.

My surgery day was actually super cool. The complexities of my case, coupled with the fact that I was at a teaching hospital, meant that I did not just have one surgeon; I had around ten surgeons, including residents. As I lay in the pre-op bed, I watched the residents gathered around the nurse's station nudge each other, saying, "No, you talk to her first." I chuckled and realized I was living my own personal, live-and-in-color episode of *Grey's Anatomy*.

The one with the most confidence, the Izzy Stevens of the bunch, came up to me and asked about my medical history. I bragged about the one-and-a-half semesters I spent pre-med in undergrad and asked her how she was enjoying OB/GYN.

"I don't—I want to be in plastics," she responded frankly. "But cases like yours are cool."

Dr. Izzy Stevens bounced back to the nurse's station and shrugged, conveying something to the effect of, "Don't worry, guys, she's cool." One by one, the doctors introduced themselves and discussed what they found fascinating or peculiar about my case.

I have to admit it's pretty cool to imagine that these poor residents were up all night studying my medical record. I started wondering how much sleep they got and hoped they were feeling awake enough to slice me open.

"Do I look way younger than you imagined?" I inquired with full transparency, expecting compliments to brighten my mood. They were pleasantly surprised by how cool, calm, and collected I was, and I quickly reminded them that this was not my first rodeo, having had multiple surgeries throughout my life.

The surgery was a quick four hours but ended up being a bit more complicated than expected. My tumor was accompanied by cysts and internal bleeding, meaning I underwent four surgeries instead of the planned one. Furthermore, because I had blood clots on multiple vital organs, the *"Grey's Anatomy"* residents were not allowed to touch me. The head surgeon performed the entire procedure on her own while they watched.

In addition to getting everything approved by my insurance company, managing to have all the receptionists squeeze me into my pre-op appointments during a busy season, and witnessing my parents act civilly toward each other, the biggest miracle of all was that my grapefruit-sized tumor turned out to be a cluster of seven smaller tumors.

I firmly believe that the Hand of God touched my tumor and shattered it into seven fragments; we had multiple ultrasounds, MRI, and CT scans from multiple angles that indicated the tumor was one, maybe two. This unexpected twist reduced the risk of leaving any rogue tissue behind and miraculously plummeted the cancer risk down to a solid zero.

I woke up after my surgery to the worst sound to have ever woken me up—my own blood-curdling screaming. First, the sound of my screams jolted me, and immediately after the pain, the excruciating pain of having been sliced and diced in twelve different ways, fileted like a fish, overwhelmed me. Nurses ran to my aid while my mother sobbed in total helplessness.

I've had multiple surgeries. In fact, I enjoy getting surgery because I usually wake up feeling like it's the best sleep I've ever had. But not this time. This time, I couldn't stop screaming; it was a solid five minutes of me begging for drugs and arguing with a nurse who refused. I'm not a drug addict, and I don't understand addiction, but at that very moment, I would have stabbed that nurse if someone had told me it would take my pain away. I'm not proud of this—it's just a fact.

Recognizing how out of character it was for me to be desperate for drugs, a glimmer of compassion for drug addicts crept into the back of my mind as I shouted, "Give me some [expletive] drugs! This pain is not normal. Call my doctor! If you don't give me drugs, I swear I will march downstairs to the tent city on La Cienega Blvd and get some myself!" A doctor came and instructed the nurse to administer morphine immediately. She did, and then I began vomiting.

Relocating to my luxury recovery suite was humiliating, painful, confusing, and awful. My recovery suite was at a swanky five-star hotel Chelsea Handler had just tagged herself on Instagram the previous evening. Before my surgery, as I packed my overnight bag, I had visions of myself in a wheelchair at the lobby bar, rolling around with celebrities recovering from some secret facelift or nose job. I had already decided that if anyone asked, I would lie and say I had gotten a BBL, which sounded way cooler than the buzzkill myomectomy I got.

I packed my makeup, hair products, and a couple of cute but comfy outfits my friend Nadine generously gifted me. It turns out I could have packed a toothbrush, toothpaste, and nothing else because that was all I used. Unable to lift my arms, my curling iron and cute, comfy clothes were useless to me. I was hooked up to IVs and couldn't even sit up, let alone use the restroom, get dressed, or hop into a wheelchair without the assistance of two people.

I required medication every hour, which left me in a perpetual state of discomfort. My pain levels fluctuated, and sleep was hard to catch as the nurses injected medication into my IV and/or arms. The most disturbing aspect was the uncharacteristic venom that spewed from my lips as I barked orders at my caregivers. I have always prided myself on treating everyone, especially healthcare providers, with unwavering respect and kindness. Now, I was morphing into a strange, bitter creature I did not recognize or like.

Incorrigible and condescending, I scolded, "Did you not read the damn notes on my chart? I am due for my antibiotics, not laxatives!" This was swiftly followed by an eruption of tears, begging for pardon and grace, as I tried to explain that I was typically a much more pleasant person than this monster that had taken hold.

For the first time in my life, my tolerance for pain, mistakes, isolation, and miscommunication was so low that I adopted a personality I did not recognize. Spinning on a merry-go-round of emotions, I felt deeply ashamed of myself as I oscillated between insulting growls and pitiful sobs. It was a frightening reminder that fear, physical pain, and loss of faculties all at once can transform a person, and I have worked very hard to forgive myself ever since.

The reaction I often receive from surgical nurses is surprise at my age, given the conditions and procedures I've undergone.

"You're so young," they say with hope and condolence.

I haven't felt young in many years; my body feels beat up after decades of being poked, prodded, sliced, diced, and sewn. Perhaps this geriatric sentiment serves me well in the corporate world, where I have always felt comfortable being the youngest in a meeting or boardroom.

I suppose now is a good time to let you know that I started writing this book from my deathbed. Greetings. My deathbed sucks. Everything hurts. How was I so naive in thinking I would be back to work in four weeks?

Ironically, I'm on bedrest during Christmas. Today doesn't look like anything I imagined, but I'm trying to stay grateful and blessed. Once again, I'm reminded that God never promised life would be perfect, easy, or painless. He promised His son, Jesus Christ, would give us everlasting life, which I suppose is the point of the whole Christmas thing.

I even bought a New Year's Eve dress because I thought I'd have time to go back and party in Dallas. What a joke—I spent NYE saying, "Hey, thanks for being here on New Year's," to the doctors, nurses, and security guards keeping watch.

One of the nurses laughed, "It's New Year's Eve? I had no idea."

I think the cruelest part of this entire experience is that as dry as my sense of humor might be, it hurts to laugh. In fact, if anybody makes me laugh, I want to punch them because it hurts that badly. It's not funny. *How did I get here?*

When I finally got to transfer from recovery back home to ride out the rest of my bed rest, I was greeted by a note that said, *"Thanks to the generosity of friends and family..."* My room had been beautifully set up with care packages, gifts, balloons, and more flowers than a funeral home.

I was despondent.

My experiences have felt so isolating because none of my friends have had the surgeries I have had. Most of my friends and family have learned about my conditions through my diagnosis.

I'm deeply grateful for the support of my loved ones and the exceptional care I've received during this challenging period. There is nothing that money could buy to make my recovery more comfortable. I have everything I need and more. And yet, I am by far the most miserable I have ever been.

I pride myself on being grateful, but I'm struggling to look past all of the things I don't have, for example, control over my body. When I finally could sit up on my own, all I did was focus on how I was unable to walk very far. And when I started walking, I was upset that I couldn't work out or run, and every time I take a step forward in my recovery, I remain plagued by the things that I am still unable to do. I pride myself on having a heart posture of gratitude, and yet, where I normally find gratitude within my heart, I now discover deep, dark bitterness.

How could God do this to me? I was so very desperate to get my life back, and in several ways, as I write this today, I still am.

Easier said than done, but I strive to have praise and gratitude in all seasons of life. I'm wise enough to know that every tear shed will rain back down like a blessing. I'm experienced enough to know that enduring pain yields tenacity, resilience, and greater consciousness. I am impatient enough to know I need more adversity to develop my patience.

My body has been through the wringer. Even watching Netflix hurts. Who knew that was possible? For perspective, while I've never experienced a cesarean section, both doctors and women who've undergone both procedures have told me that the myomectomy I had is notably more painful than a C-section. I can't help but feel a mix of frustration and disbelief. All I want to do at the moment is be able to walk at a normal pace. I don't know, maybe pee by myself, not have to wear a diaper. *Nobody mentioned that I'd be wearing a diaper!*

I am stuck. (Tick tock.) What I really want to do so badly is astral-project. I can't count how many times I have begged in the last few weeks, "Lord, I don't care if you turn me into the telephone pole up the road. I just have to get out of this body, this flesh prison. I am in so much pain. I don't want to be here anymore. Hello? Can you hear me?"

My days are almost exactly the same. And if this whole life thing were a video game, I would do a hard reset because it's the worst version ever (Control, Alt, Delete). What makes me feel even worse is that I have it so easy, and yet this feels so hard. I got to spend my post-op in the same recovery suite where celebrities heal from their plastic surgery away from the paparazzi. I received care from the best hospital in the world, Cedars-Sinai, the same place that delivered Beyoncé's twin babies.

Okay, that's a Los Angeles urban legend and not actually true. But if Angelinos want to perpetuate this lie, I won't correct them. I have 24-hour care, delicious home-cooked meals, and a tribe that loves me. But I can't really enjoy any of it because I'm so sick and in so much pain. I have it as good as anyone could have it, yet I am utterly miserable.

I am hyper-aware. I shouldn't complain because what I have experienced in the past few weeks can only be described as miraculous. I have always been a woman of faith, but this has been the first time I asked for prayers and miracles, and He delivered.

I've had multiple surgeries throughout my life, and the scary part is they are not getting easier. It took me a full week before I had the nerve (and strength) to stand up and look at my body in the mirror. I never realized how much I liked my belly button, and now, every time I look at it and all of its deformed glory, I wonder how something so insignificant can have such an impact on my self-esteem.

My boss calls to ask quick questions about outstanding items at work and when I plan to return. *Does he realize I am soaking in blood-stained sheets right now?* As I tried to convey to my doctors, this whole ordeal could not have come at a less convenient time. Roughly 30 to 50% of alcohol sales occur in OND (October, November, December), with each month's sales doubling the previous volume.

Imagine the juxtaposition of me screaming in agony and pain and then picking up the phone to answer questions about a delayed vodka delivery for one of our retailers. Between quick work calls from colleagues, I am waddling to the bathroom, dripping blood on the floor. My recovery takes longer than expected, and eventually, my boss informs me they have to let me go right before Christmas—'tis the season.

Word spreads about my job vacancy, and I receive inquiries from competitive brands regarding potential job opportunities. A prominent beer company is seeking a manager for a multicultural program for their latest seltzer line, while a whiskey manufacturer is interested in revitalizing their previously unsuccessful canned-cocktail innovation. Additionally, a tequila brand I've previously worked for asks if I'd be willing to relocate to Canada for a VP of Sales role. I try to answer these emails and calls when possible but politely decline video conferences. I'd rather not have to explain why I am propped up in my bed, naked and pale.

Moving anything other than my thumbs and neck sends waves of excruciating pain through my body. I find myself in a profound moment of self-reflection: *why am I sacrificing my physical health to discuss sales and marketing strategies for alcohol companies?* The exhaustion I feel, the deep weariness that has settled in, has led me to question whether I can continue dedicating my life, my heart, my blood, sweat, and tears to this industry any longer.

Throughout my career in alcohol sales and marketing, I've played an instrumental role in generating over $1 billion in revenue for a diverse range of clients and partners, spanning from Fortune 500 brands to innovative startups and nonprofits. I have dared to dream that I could be the woman who smashes glass ceilings, scaling the ranks from promo model to executive, challenging the objectification of women synonymous with alcohol advertising for so long. Despite the challenges inherent in an industry often associated with vices, I've cherished the opportunities to craft moments of joy and cultivate positive working environments for people. With plans of spending my golden years bartending at a vacation resort, I genuinely saw myself working in the "booze biz" for the rest of my life.

However, as I find myself fielding calls about beer, whiskey, and delayed vodka deliveries from my bed, this career that was once a source of exhilaration and accomplishment seems to contrast with my newfound desire to prioritize my physical health and well-being.

Lacking the conventional roles of motherhood or marriage that most women my age seem to have, I'm compelled to confront the notion of my identity without this career. *Who am I without it, and can I start anew?*

Lying in bed, typing this chapter on my phone, I am drained. Medical bills wait for no one. With my sheets and diaper drenched in blood and my savings account steadily diminishing, I find myself bleeding out both physically and financially—dual hemorrhages. Grateful to enjoy television again, I rewatched the movie *Juno*, which always made me laugh in my younger years. While watching the title character go into labor (spoiler alert: she eventually has the baby), a thought crossed my mind. *I wonder if I'll scream like that during labor.* But then, I remind myself I'll never experience childbirth like that. Because of the trauma my body has endured, I am ineligible for a natural birth. Should I ever be blessed enough to experience a full-term pregnancy, it's "C-section city" for me, with a side of high risk. I still don't know how I feel about that, and I can only hope my future husband doesn't mind.

The fall season has always been my favorite, but this one has been particularly hard to navigate. I recently learned about the phenomenon of why leaves fall before winter comes. I had always assumed the leaves fell because they got too cold and died. I was fascinated to learn that falling leaves play a crucial role in the health and survival of trees.

Trees shed their leaves to conserve energy and water and to prevent heavy snow buildup that could snap their branches. Similarly, there are moments in life when our own leaves must be stripped away to avoid being broken by the weight of our burdens. In this period of stillness and loss, I sense that much is being taken from me in preparation for a season of renewal and growth.

CHAPTER TEN

Life After Alcohol: Finding Purpose Beyond the Bottle

"You really suck at unemployment, you know that, right?" a friend taunted.

I chuckled, then groaned, "Don't make me laugh, or I'll kill you."

Although laughing still hurts and my belly button remains disfigured, I am gradually recovering, rearranging my life piece by piece. Forced to do a hard reset, I've been deeply reflecting on my new life outside the alcohol industry. Prayerfully, my robust career has afforded me the opportunity to take the year off and rediscover myself. I graduated from college on a high horse, proud of myself for having jobs lined up and thus avoiding some of the career uncertainty and financial concerns my peers endured. Yet, here I am, several years later, in a very similar boat—the irony of my pride before the fall is not lost upon me.

I'm catching a glimpse of what retirement might feel like, stepping away from the daily grind of work and obligations and relying on my savings and the help of family. I've also been pensive about my accomplishments and where my life is headed—facing your mortality will do that to you. This experience of being bedridden, unable to work, relying on others for help, and enduring agonizing pain has given me a preview of what the end of the road looks like for many of us.

If retirement mirrors this experience, I can confidently declare that the pride you derive from investing in your development, your family, your friends, and your community will undoubtedly transcend any accomplishments of your career. My ability to take a sabbatical year is a privilege and the result of decades of sound financial planning, diligence, creating opportunities, risk-taking, late nights, and being productive. But ultimately, our jobs and employers can do something our families cannot—replace us when we get sick and die. Despite my ongoing physical challenges and preoccupation with my fertility and mortality, there's hope for my improvement. It is not lost on me that this hope is a privilege that the elderly are denied in their final days.

This season of my mini-retirement reminds me of the story of the businessman and the fisherman.

One day, a businessman went on vacation and saw a fisherman sitting on a boat, fishing with a pole. The businessman said to the fisherman, "You could make more money catching fish if you used a net instead of a pole."

The fisherman probed, "Okay, and then what would I do?"

The businessman replied, "Well, from there, you could start selling a bunch of fish."

"Okay, and then what would I do?" asked the fisherman.

The businessman continued, "You could buy a bigger boat with the money you make, and with a bigger boat, you can catch more fish.

Eventually, you'll be able to buy a bunch of boats all over the world and have your employees catch fish for you."

To which the fisherman inquired, "Okay, and then what would my reward for that be?"

A little frustrated, the businessman answered, "Don't you understand? You'll become so rich that you'll never have to work for a living again. You can spend your days sitting on a beach, looking at a sunset without a care in the world."

The fisherman looked up and smiled, "Isn't that what I'm doing right now?"

This time off has allowed me to redirect my life, travel a bit, volunteer, write this book, relaunch my podcast *Eavesdrop with Ella*, and finally explore passions I've always held but never had the chance to pursue. I've attended seminars on Artificial Intelligence, Cybersecurity, and tax-free accounts. I've also started investing in real estate, consulting for small businesses, attending church, rejoining my Bible study, and volunteering. As I was handing out food downtown, a homeless man hit on me, and all I could think was, *If only he knew I was wearing a diaper right now.*

As I delve into existential contemplations, a profound question persists: *Who am I in the absence of work?* Sick in bed, barely able to sit up, wearing a diaper, and hopped up on 13 different drugs (and not the fun ones), I yearn for an escape. With no career, husband, child, or milestones on the horizon to distract me, I decided to book a solo trip to Europe, against the advice of my doctors and close family, in pursuit of physical renewal and rediscovering joy.

"As you travel around, marveling, remember that God made all that beauty, looked at the world, and decided it needed you too," my friend Racquel—aka @itstheracq—generously reminds me as I globe-trot across Europe.

As I explore Europe, I cry every day. Sometimes they are happy tears, sometimes sad. These words keep repeating in my head: *Thank You, God. You are so good. Thank you for my ability to walk. Thank you for the hair that keeps blowing in my mouth and eyes. Thank you for my sunburn. Thank you for my body odor. Thank you, thank you, thank you.*

Writing parts of this book from the canals of Amsterdam, the beaches of Croatia, and historic rooftops in Greece is even more magical, healing, and transformative than I had envisioned. Nevertheless, even halfway around the world, I am still plagued by the same question, "So, what do you do?"

Working in alcohol sales and marketing was never just a job for me; it's how I have introduced myself to others for years. Leaving that behind makes me feel like I'm losing a fundamental part of who I am. I have almost perfected my spiel, my elevator pitch, which explains that I am rediscovering my true self beyond a bottle of booze. I'm not just pursuing a new path but also redefining my identity on my own terms.

I've always believed that **your career should be at the intersection where your passion meets profit**. My passion is people— interacting with people, creating experiences, educating, inspiring, and helping people. So, choosing a career in wine and spirits felt fitting—where people gather alcohol often follows.

Alcohol's powerful grip is challenging to escape, interwoven into several aspects of my life. Even when I don't plan to buy any alcoholic beverages, I'm instinctively attracted to the aisles displaying wine, beer, or liquor whenever I'm shopping. I navigate these sections out of habit, taking note of market trends and promotional strategies. Similarly, when I walk into a bar or restaurant, my eyes scan the menu to identify brands and partners. I think to myself, *The Bar in Dubrovnik, Croatia, clearly has an affiliation with Diageo.* This constant exposure to alcohol marketing efforts is a reminder of how deeply ingrained it has been in my career and personal experiences. Stepping away from a career I have built for over 18 years is no simple feat. My finances are uncertain if I start from scratch somewhere else, and I don't feel particularly young enough to learn new tricks. Pragmatically, I know that the self-doubt that creeps in, although entirely normal, is wrong.

Understandably, many of us would stay exactly where we are, feeling stuck on our plateau, unable to imagine starting anew. Fear of change, fear of failure, or just a lack of confidence often hinder us from pursuing the exciting life we all deserve. To overcome this, we can build confidence by taking small actions, small steps toward an achievable goal. My career began with applying to fast-food restaurants and getting rejected repeatedly. Throughout my various roles, friends and mentors have recognized my hard work and helped pave new pathways for me.

Whether I was crafting multi-million-dollar marketing campaigns, motivating sales teams, or mentoring individuals one-on-one, my unwavering passion has always been to engage with and uplift others.

Urban legends suggest that drunk people sustain fewer injuries in car accidents because their bodies are more relaxed—they don't resist. There's a certain wisdom in the art of flowing and letting go, even though it's something I've found uncomfortable at times.

I have built a career by bending over backward, saying yes to others, and embracing change and challenges. "Yes, I will relocate across the country to build your business." "Yes, I will endure late nights and the frustrations that come with them." "Yes, I will brave uncomfortable conversations and untangle the messes you've created." "Yes, I will faithfully uphold the confidentiality of your business practices."

I feel deep gratitude for the unforgettable relationships, network, personal growth, insights, fortitude, and cultural awareness this career has afforded me. Designing advertisements and watching the brands I've helped build thrive has been remarkable. I will always be thankful for my time in this industry because it has provided me with invaluable lessons that I will carry into my future endeavors:

- ❖ **"Your reputation matters."**
- ❖ **"The riches are in the niches."**
- ❖ **"What made you successful today might not be enough to make you successful tomorrow."**
- ❖ **"Be quick to apologize."**
- ❖ **"In business, everyone is held accountable to someone."**
- ❖ **"Your career should be the intersection of where your passion meets profit."**

After 15 rewarding years in alcohol sales and marketing, I'm ready to embark on a transformative career shift driven by a desire to positively impact lives. Clearly, my recent health challenges have been a catalyst for this transformation, forcing me to confront a reckoning within. While I don't know the details of my next chapter, either metaphorically or literally, I do know that I aim to inspire others to navigate life's inevitable challenges with brilliance and resilience, continuing a legacy of compassion and empowerment.

I am working to build a new career path that will allow me to focus on spiritual, emotional, financial, and physical goals. For now, I'm just taking it one day at a time, rebuilding my career, my stability, and my confidence brick by brick.

Much like when I was choosing a college major, I'm driven by a myriad of interests, including real estate investing, technology, acquiring coaching certifications, and volunteering with young adults from the foster care system.

As I step into the unknown, armed with resilience and motivation, I am thrilled to discover where my passions may lead me next.

THANK YOU!

Thank you once again for being a part of this book's success.

I truly hope you've discovered valuable insights that resonate with your own pursuit of a more balanced and fulfilling life.

My mission is to assist others in reshaping their perspectives on success in all aspects of life.

Your input is incredibly valuable to me. Please don't hesitate to reach out through ellayourbella.com and share your thoughts by rating and reviewing the book on platforms like Amazon.com.

Your feedback fuels my work and plays a pivotal role in shaping future projects.

Thank you for your support!

With heartfelt wishes for your self-care and alignment,

Ella